BIOTERRORISM: ASSESSING THE THREAT

HEARING

BEFORE THE

SUBCOMMITTEE ON EMERGENCY PREPAREDNESS, RESPONSE, AND COMMUNICATIONS

OF THE

COMMITTEE ON HOMELAND SECURITY HOUSE OF REPRESENTATIVES

ONE HUNDRED THIRTEENTH CONGRESS

SECOND SESSION

FEBRUARY 11, 2014

Serial No. 113–51

Printed for the use of the Committee on Homeland Security

Available via the World Wide Web: http://www.gpo.gov/fdsys/

U.S. GOVERNMENT PRINTING OFFICE

88–168 PDF   WASHINGTON : 2014

For sale by the Superintendent of Documents, U.S. Government Printing Office
Internet: bookstore.gpo.gov   Phone: toll free (866) 512–1800; DC area (202) 512–1800
Fax: (202) 512–2250   Mail: Stop SSOP, Washington, DC 20402–0001

COMMITTEE ON HOMELAND SECURITY

MICHAEL T. MCCAUL, Texas, *Chairman*

LAMAR SMITH, Texas
PETER T. KING, New York
MIKE ROGERS, Alabama
PAUL C. BROUN, Georgia
CANDICE S. MILLER, Michigan, *Vice Chair*
PATRICK MEEHAN, Pennsylvania
JEFF DUNCAN, South Carolina
TOM MARINO, Pennsylvania
JASON CHAFFETZ, Utah
STEVEN M. PALAZZO, Mississippi
LOU BARLETTA, Pennsylvania
RICHARD HUDSON, North Carolina
STEVE DAINES, Montana
SUSAN W. BROOKS, Indiana
SCOTT PERRY, Pennsylvania
MARK SANFORD, South Carolina
VACANCY

BENNIE G. THOMPSON, Mississippi
LORETTA SANCHEZ, California
SHEILA JACKSON LEE, Texas
YVETTE D. CLARKE, New York
BRIAN HIGGINS, New York
CEDRIC L. RICHMOND, Louisiana
WILLIAM R. KEATING, Massachusetts
RON BARBER, Arizona
DONALD M. PAYNE, JR., New Jersey
BETO O'ROURKE, Texas
TULSI GABBARD, Hawaii
FILEMON VELA, Texas
STEVEN A. HORSFORD, Nevada
ERIC SWALWELL, California

VACANCY, *Staff Director*
MICHAEL GEFFROY, *Deputy Staff Director/Chief Counsel*
MICHAEL S. TWINCHEK, *Chief Clerk*
I. LANIER AVANT, *Minority Staff Director*

————

SUBCOMMITTEE ON EMERGENCY PREPAREDNESS, RESPONSE, AND COMMUNICATIONS

SUSAN W. BROOKS, Indiana, *Chairwoman*

PETER T. KING, New York
STEVEN M. PALAZZO, Mississippi, *Vice Chair*
SCOTT PERRY, Pennsylvania
MARK SANFORD, South Carolina
MICHAEL T. MCCAUL, Texas *(ex officio)*

DONALD M. PAYNE, JR., New Jersey
YVETTE D. CLARKE, New York
BRIAN HIGGINS, New York
BENNIE G. THOMPSON, Mississippi *(ex officio)*

ERIC B. HEIGHBERGER, *Subcommittee Staff Director*
DEBORAH JORDAN, *Subcommittee Clerk*

CONTENTS

BIOTERRORISM: ASSESSING THE THREAT

Tuesday, February 11, 2014

U.S. HOUSE OF REPRESENTATIVES,
SUBCOMMITTEE ON EMERGENCY PREPAREDNESS,
RESPONSE, AND COMMUNICATIONS,
COMMITTEE ON HOMELAND SECURITY,
Washington, DC.

The subcommittee met, pursuant to call, at 10:05 a.m., in Room 311, Cannon House Office Building, Hon. Susan W. Brooks [Chairwoman of the subcommittee] presiding.

Present: Representatives Brooks, King, Palazzo, Perry, Sanford, Payne, Clarke, Higgins, and Thompson (ex officio).

Also present: Representative Pascrell.

Mrs. BROOKS. The Subcommittee on Emergency Preparedness, Response, and Communications will come to order. The subcommittee is meeting today to receive testimony on the threat of bioterrorism.

Mr. PAYNE. Madam Chairwoman, I ask unanimous consent that the gentleman from New Jersey, Mr. Pascrell, be allowed to sit for the purpose of questioning the witnesses at our hearing today.

Mrs. BROOKS. Without objection, so ordered.

Today's hearing is part of the oversight work this subcommittee has conducted and will be conducting on bioterrorism and the Department of Homeland Security's biosurveillance capabilities. As a former U.S. Attorney for the Southern District of the Indiana appointed in October 2001, I was involved in the National response and alert surrounding the anthrax attacks in 2001. We know that while it has been more than a decade, we still need to be reminded that these attacks killed 5 people and sickened at least 20 others. These attacks showed us both the physical and psychological impacts of a bioterrorism event and they were a reminder that a small amount of a biological agent can have a large impact.

In his 2003 report, "Catastrophic Bioterrorism, What is to Be Done," Richard Danzig noted that the 1 gram of anthrax, which I might note is about a sugar-packet size, was sent to Senator Leahy, it contained a trillion spores, an amount that if effectively dispersed, could kill thousands of people and could cause great economic damage. I don't say this to be an alarmist, but we must be aware of all of the threats that we face. I fear that over the course of time, people have lost sight of the potential impacts of such an attack and why we must remain vigilant and prepared, and because of this, I think this hearing is very important to, again, talk about this threat and what we are doing about it.

(1)

In addition to this hearing, the subcommittee is also doing several other activities surrounding bioterrorism and biosurveillance. At the request of Ranking Member Payne and myself, as well as the Chairman and Ranking Member of the full committee, the GAO is conducting a review of the National Biosurveillance Integration Center to determine whether the NBIC is working to its potential, whether it is providing value to the Federal participants and whether it continues to be worthy of our vital National security dollars. The subcommittee is also continuing its oversight of the BioWatch program, the Office of Health Affairs' flagship program designed to detect aerosolized bioterror agents.

BioWatch is at a crossroads, and Members may recall that this subcommittee requested a GAO review of the program in 112th Congress, which was released in September 2012. Among its recommendations was that the Department complete an analysis of alternatives for the Generation III, or Gen–3, system to determine whether or not this approach is the right way to go, and the Institute for Defense Analysis completed this analysis and delivered the results to the Department late last year. It is my understanding that the Department is currently reviewing the AOA and considering options for the future of the program.

I urge them, and as we will discuss with Secretary Johnson who will be before us tomorrow, before the full committee, to thoughtfully consider the results of the AOA to determine the most appropriate path forward for the BioWatch program. I look forward to receiving testimony from the Department on this issue in the near future.

As the foundation of this future work, we are meeting today to receive an update on the bioterrorism threat, and we know the threat is real. In testimony before this subcommittee in the 112th Congress, former Senator Jim Talent, vice chair of the WMD Commission reminded us of the Commission's finding that it was likely that there would be an WMD attack somewhere in the world by the end of 2013 and that, in their judgment, the attack was more likely to be biological.

Bioweapons can be developed surreptitiously, transported with relative ease and deployed insidiously over time. Obviously, as we all know, the attack in Syria was just that sort of an attack, with respect to an attack that the WMD Commission predicted.

We have no reason to believe that the threat has changed since that testimony. In materials prepared for his appearance before the House Intelligence Committee just last week, Director of National Intelligence, James Clapper, noted that the intelligence community remains focused on the proliferation of chemical and biological warfare-related materials and development of WMD delivery systems.

In addition to nation-state actors, the intelligence community has also judged that groups like al-Qaeda and its affiliates are intent on conducting CBRN attacks against the United States. So, I am pleased that we will be receiving testimony from such a distinguished panel of witnesses today to put this threat into perspective. I will note for the Members that we are planning to follow up this hearing with a Classified briefing on the threat later this month, and with that, I look forward to the testimony and our discussion here this morning.

The Chairwoman now recognizes the gentleman from New Jersey, our Ranking Member, Mr. Payne, for any opening statement he may have.

Mr. PAYNE. Good morning. First, I would like to thank Chairwoman Brooks for holding the hearing today on the threats posed by bioterrorism. I would also like to thank Chairwoman Brooks for allowing my friend and my colleague, my mentor from the Garden State, Congressman Bill Pascrell, to participate in today's important hearing. As a former Member of the committee and a leader on bioterrorism issues, I know we will benefit from his expertise.

I commend Mr.—I commend both Mr. Pascrell and Mr. King, the lead sponsors on the WMD Prevention and Preparedness Act, for their efforts to comprehensively address the threats that are posed by weapons of mass destruction, particularly biological weapons. I admire their bipartisan effort and their persistence in championing this legislation that will implement many of the recommendations of the bipartisan WMD Commission. I look forward to doing my part to help advance the bill.

As a freshman Member, I appreciate this opportunity to explore threats posed by weapons, weaponized pathogens, and what we can do as legislators to address them. During my preparation for this hearing, two things stuck out to me. First, without a special assistant to the President for biodefense, there does not appear to be a unified coordinated effort for addressing these threats posed by biological weapons.

Second, we are not where we need to be with respect to caring for children in the event of a biological attack.

To my first point, it seems that the Federal effort to address bioterrorism ebbs and flows. In December 2009, President Obama signed an Executive Order that outlined a process for the Federal Government to deliver medical countermeasures. Shortly after the administration created a Federal working group tasked with designating this high-risk Tier 1 biological select agents and toxins, the release in July 2012 of National strategy on biosurveillance—biosurveillance that emphasized the need to coordinate among Federal, State, and local governments, the private sector was a really positive step.

However, since that time, specifics on how to carry out the strategy have not been forthcoming. As a result, efforts continue to be disjointed. I am not alone in reaching this conclusion. GAO stated in its testimony before this subcommittee in 2012 that the National biosurveillance efforts continue to be without a system to determine current resources, ask assessed risk, and prioritize investment. This mission is too critical to be without a coordinated and consistent Federal framework.

To my second point, I am concerned, as a Nation, we have not done enough to ensure in the event of a biological attack, children get the care that they need. It is well-understood that as a population, children may experience biological reactions to weaponized pathogens more quickly than adults. There is a very healthy and active debate about the development and provision of countermeasures to children.

Last April, the GAO reported that 40 percent of countermeasures in the strategic National stockpile were not approved for the use on children. I understand that last—I understand that last year, the President's Commission for the study on biological—bioethical issues released a report entitled, "Safeguarding Children, Pediatric Countermeasures Research" to make recommendations about carrying out research for medical countermeasures for children.

Aside from the question of developing and stockpiling countermeasures for children, there is the matter of treating children in such a disaster. I am concerned that in recent years, the advent of the Federal support for public health such as a termination of funding for the Metropolitan Medical Response System and its vital programs, local public health personnel do not have the training necessary to treat the unique needs of children who have been exposed to weaponized pathogens. I look forward to learning more about these issues from our witnesses.

I want to thank the witnesses for being here today, and I look forward to their testimony, and I yield back. But Madam Chairwoman, before I yield back—that was in the script, but before I yield back, you know, I had a situation when I was president of the Newark Municipal Council that an envelope was mailed to my home and mailed to several other council members during our tenure, and one of my children's jobs is to get the mail. Luckily, this day, my wife picked the mail up and a powdery substance had been mailed to my home and several other council members. The other council members, it was mailed to City Hall, but this one was mailed to my home.

So, you know, I have an experience with what this could potentially be and mean to citizens that we are here to protect and serve, so I just wanted to add that, that this is very, very important work we are doing and the witnesses and very personal to me and what it means to children. Thank you.

[The statement of Ranking Member Payne follows:]

STATEMENT OF RANKING MEMBER DONALD M. PAYNE, JR.

FEBRUARY 11, 2014

As a former Member of the Committee, and a leader on bioterrorism issues, I know we will all benefit from his expertise. I commend both Mr. Pascrell and Mr. King—the lead sponsors of "the WMD Prevention and Preparedness Act"—for their efforts to comprehensively address the threats posed by Weapons of Mass Destruction—particularly biological weapons. I admire their bipartisan effort—and persistence—in championing legislation that will implement many of the recommendations of the bipartisan WMD Commission. I look forward to doing my part to help advance the bill.

As a Freshman Member, I appreciate this opportunity to explore the threats posed by weaponized pathogens and what we can do, as legislators, to address them. During my preparation for this hearing, two things stuck out to me. First, without a special assistant to the President for biodefense, there does not appear to be a unified, coordinated effort for addressing the threats posed by biological weapons. Second, we are not where we need to be with respect to caring for children in the event of a biological attack.

To my first point, it seems that the Federal effort to address bio-terrorism ebbs and flows. In December 2009, President Obama signed an Executive Order that outlined a process for the Federal Government to deliver medical countermeasures. Shortly thereafter, the administration created a Federal working group tasked with designating the highest risk or "Tier 1" biological select agents and toxins.

The release, in July 2012, of a *National Strategy on Biosurveillance* that emphasized the need to coordinate among Federal, State, and local governments and the private sector was a positive step. However, since that time, specifics on how to carry out the Strategy have not been forthcoming. As a result, efforts continue to be disjointed.

I am not alone in reaching this conclusion, GAO stated in its testimony before this subcommittee in 2012 that National biosurveillance efforts continue to be without a system to determine current resources, assess risk, and prioritize investments. This mission is too critical to be without a coordinated and consistent Federal framework.

To my second point, I am concerned that, as a Nation, we have not done enough to ensure that, in the event of a biological attack, children get the care they need. It is well-understood that, as a population, children may experience biological reactions to weaponized pathogens more quickly than adults.

There is a very healthy and active debate about the development and provision of countermeasures to children. Last April, the GAO reported that 40 percent of the countermeasures in the Strategic National Stockpile were not approved for use on children. I understand that, last year, the President's Commission for the Study of Bioethical Issues released a report entitled *Safeguarding Children: Pediatric Countermeasure Research,* to make recommendations about carrying out research for medical countermeasures for children. Aside from the questions of developing and stockpiling countermeasures for children, there is the matter of treating children in such a disaster.

I am concerned that, in recent years, the advent of less Federal support for public health—such as the termination of funding for the Metropolitan Medical Response System and other vital programs—local public health personnel do not have the training necessary to treat the unique needs of children who have been exposed to weaponized pathogens. I look forward to learning more about these issues from our witnesses.

Mrs. BROOKS. Thank you, Congressman Payne, and thanks for reminding me that we also had an incident when I was U.S. Attorney a couple—I think on more than one occasion where letters were mailed to our office as Federal employees and with powder and the office had to go through the emergency procedures and HAZMAT teams were called to test it and so forth, and so—and you know, we just saw very recently what happened in Sochi, or I am sorry, at the Super Bowl, rather, with hotels, with powder being sent to various hotels, and so, I think you reminded us of the psychological impact and the fear that doing something as simple as going and getting the mail can have on your family, so thank you for sharing that.

Members are reminded that additional statements may be submitted for the record.

[The statement of Ranking Member Thompson follows:]

STATEMENT OF RANKING MEMBER BENNIE G. THOMPSON

FEBRUARY 11, 2014

I understand that Congressman Pascrell and Congressman King plan to reintroduce the WMD Prevention and Preparedness Act today. I commend both of them on their efforts to improve WMD preparedness, response, and recovery in a bipartisan manner.

Their bill has been approved by the full committee twice. With any luck, maybe the third time will be the charm, and this critical legislation will finally get due consideration by the full House. Enactment of this measure will strengthen our Nation's homeland security posture in very meaningful ways—particularly in the area of bio-defense.

Over the past 10 years, we have invested over $60 billion in bio-security programs. Nevertheless, most of the assessments I have seen indicate that the United States is not where it needs to be with respect to preventing and responding to a large-scale biological attack. The legislation authored by Mr. Pascrell and Mr. King would begin the effort of building a robust biodefense enterprise.

In addition, it would ensure that first responders have the committed and collaborative Federal partner needed to address the unique issues of a potential WMD attack.

Importantly, the bill reauthorizes the Metropolitan Medical Response System (MMRS). This critical grant program has not been funded since 2011, and its authorization has lapsed. The MMRS reauthorization language included in this bill would provide grants to metropolitan areas to bolster medical surge capacity, strengthen capabilities, and improve biological response and decontamination activities.

State and local public health departments have been hit hard by budget cuts, and they need MMRS. I am committed to seeing the WMD bill become law, but I know there are obstacles in its path. As we work to resolve those issues, I hope that the legislation can be the springboard for discussion, and that it will keep the issue of biodefense and WMD on the front burner. I thank the witnesses for being here, and I look forward to their testimony.

Mrs. BROOKS. We are pleased this morning to have a very distinguished panel before us on this important topic. Dr. Robert Kadlec served 26 years as an officer and physician in the United States Air Force where he held senior positions in the Executive and Legislative branches. Until January 2009, Dr. Kadlec served as the special assistant to the President and senior director for biodefense policy on the Homeland Security Council. While on the Homeland Security Council, Dr. Kadlec drafted the National Biodefense Policy for the 21st Century, which became Homeland Security Presidential Policy Directive 10. He was also the staff director of the Senate Committee on Health, Education, Labor, and Pension's Subcommittee for Bioterrorism and Public Health Preparedness.

Next is Dr. Tom Inglesby, who is the director of the UPMC Center for Health Security. He serves as a co-chair of the National Health Security Preparedness Index Initiative and has also been a chair or a member of a number of National Academy of Sciences committees. He is coeditor-in-chief of the journal *Biosecurity and Bioterrorism: Biodefense Strategy, Practice and Science* and is an associate professor of medicine and public health at the University of Pittsburgh Schools of Medicine and Public Health. I now yield to the Ranking Member to introduce our next witness.

Mr. PAYNE. Thank you, Madam Chairwoman. I am pleased to introduce Dr. Leonard Cole, an expert on bioterrorism and on terror medicine. Dr. Cole is an adjunct professor at the University of Medicine and Dentistry of New Jersey, where he is the director on the program of terror medicine and security, which is part of the University's centers for biodefense. Dr. Cole serves on the advisory board of the International Institute of Counterterrorism and is a trustee of the Washington Institute for Near East Policy.

He has written numerous articles for professional journals as well as general publications, including *The New York Times, Washington Post, Scientific American,* and the *Sciences*.

Let's see. Dr. Cole received a BA with the highest honors from University of California at Berkley. He holds a master's degree and Ph.D. in political science from Columbia University and a doctorate from the University of Pennsylvania School of Dental Medicine, which in 2008 awarded him its alumni award of merit. We are happy to have him testify before us, the committee today.

Mrs. BROOKS. Thank you. Just to remind you as witnesses before us, it is a green, yellow, red light, and the green will go on when you begin testifying and the yellow light comes on when you have a minute left in your testimony, and so if you could do your best to wrap up in that last minute, that would be terrific so we can hear from all of you.

So the full written statements will appear in the record, and we appreciate the time and effort that went into preparing those full written statements, and the Chairwoman now recognizes Dr. Kadlec for 5 minutes.

STATEMENT OF ROBERT P. KADLEC, FORMER SPECIAL ASSISTANT TO THE PRESIDENT FOR BIODEFENSE

Dr. KADLEC. Thank you, Madam Chairwoman Brooks and Ranking Member Payne. It is a privilege to appear before you today, and Members of the subcommittee, to talk about this serious National security issue. It doesn't receive the kind of attention or consideration that it deserves. I would like to commend the committee for taking the time and effort to raise awareness and inform the public about it.

Congress plays a vital leadership role through hearings like this authorizing important programs and appropriating sufficient funds to ensure the means to protect America and Americans from this threat. The risk of BW's attacks is not an easy problem to talk about. Frankly, it scares people. The deliberate use of biological agents or toxins is as distinct from natural diseases and highlights a fundamental principle not found in nature, the efforts of a thinking enemy to inflict death, incapacitation, or economic loss by confounding diagnosis and frustrating treatment.

Adversaries who use BW are intent on creating conditions that are not found in nature, aerosolizing overwhelming doses to infect large numbers of people with agents that are more virulent than natural strains and resistant to common forms of treatment.

Conflating deliberate and natural infectious diseases implies that by addressing the more common natural problem, the solution will be sufficient to address the BW threat. It is not. To confront this threat effectively requires an understanding of its fundamental principle, and I am afraid we have not done so yet. It is a threat that could result in a significant loss of life, severe economic losses, and cause social instability and forever change our way of life. Simply stated, BW can kill as many people or more than the nuclear weapon. The technological barriers to achieve this potential are significantly less for nuclear weapons. Graham Allison, the founding dean of Harvard's John F. Kennedy School of Government and a leader and an expert on nuclear proliferation said, "Nuclear terrorism is a preventable catastrophe, and the reason it is preventable is because the material to make a nuclear bomb can't be made by terrorists. Can I prevent terrorists from getting it into their hands anthrax or other pathogens? No. Even our best efforts can't do that. The fact that it has not yet happened may be luck that is undoubtedly assisted by the efforts of the U.S. military intelligence community disrupting terrorist groups."

Madam Chairwoman, I think you noted the testimony by national—Director of National Intelligence, James Clapper, that starkly conveyed the reality that we find ourselves in. The global trends emerging for the risk of BW are alarming, and in addition to those that he outlined in terms of the dual-use nature of this technology diffusing globally, complicating this picture is the discipline of synthetic biology. The World Health Organization has assessed that advances in synthetic biology now permits adversaries to recreate pathogens no longer found in nature such as smallpox. General Clapper also noted that elements of serious BW program might have progressed beyond research and development, and might have achieved limited agent production. In an environment where a variety of radical Islamic groups, some aligned with al-Qaeda, the risk that 1 or 2 kilograms of anthrax could fall into the hands of terrorists should motivate us significantly to improve our preparedness.

During my tenure as a special assistant to the President, we evaluated and modeled the human and economic impact that a couple of grams, kilograms of anthrax could have on a major metropolitan area. Such an attack could threaten millions, kill several hundred thousand, and result in a direct economic impact of greater than $1 trillion.

As good as our intelligence is, it can never be perfect. The 2005 Commission on the Intelligence Capabilities of the United States regarding WMD characterized the biological threat has the greatest intelligence challenge. According to a senior CIA official interviewed for that report, we don't know more about the BW threat than we did 5 years ago, and 5 years from now, we will know even less.

Our intelligence was less than perfect in identifying the al-Qaeda clandestine BW weapons laboratory in Afghanistan prior to the invasion of the United States in the 2002. The possibility and probability that al-Qaeda may still harbor the strategic intent and may still pursue BW capabilities to attack the United States should be sufficient impetus. The risk of surprise is great and more preparedness, not less, is our greatest insurance policy. It requires a champion in Congress and in the White House and continued support of programs like BioWatch, the biothreat risk assessment, National Biodefense Analysis and Countermeasures Center, as well as programs at HHS for biosurveillance, BARDA, BioShield, and Strategic National Stockpile.

Finally, it also requires promoting vaccinations of first responders against the most likely biological threats and means for home medical kids to protect first responders and their families. The risk of bioattacks in the United States is an uncertain yet imminent reality. It requires a credible and rapid means to detect, mitigate such attacks, and equally credible means to attribute and hold those accountable. I thank you for this opportunity and look forward to your questions.

[The prepared statement of Dr. Kadlec follows:]

PREPARED STATEMENT OF ROBERT P. KADLEC

FEBRUARY 11, 2014

Madame Chairwoman Brooks and Ranking Member Payne it is a privilege and honor to appear before you and Members of this subcommittee to talk about a very important National security issue: Bioterrorism and biological warfare. It is a subject that has not received the kind of attention or consideration that it deserves and I would like to commend the committee for taking the time and effort to raise awareness and inform the public about it. Congress plays a vital role in confronting this threat through hearings like this, authorizing important programs, and appropriating the necessary funds to ensure we have the means and medical countermeasures to deter and if necessary protect America and Americans from this threat.

Talking about the threat I am always reminded of the sage words of Dr. Joshua Lederberg, Nobel Prize-winning microbiologist who said "I am very worried about this (bioterrorism) but hardly dare to mention it for fear of putting an evil idea in someone's head." His words resonant constantly with me and serve as a practical warning. But, the practical reality argues that in a democracy we must talk about these otherwise unspeakable threats in a responsible way to inform, not to incite. If no one talks about the risks of biowarfare (BW) or bioterrorism (BT); few in Government will think about it, much less act to do the necessary things to protect America and Americans.

The risk of deliberate biological attacks is not an easy problem to talk about. Frankly, it scares people. In today's public discourse, we usually hear the risk embedded in the phrase natural, accidental, and deliberate disease threats.

Somehow if we cloak it with other infectious disease threats that emerge from Mother Nature it is easier to contemplate or accept. We do ourselves, however, a great disservice by doing so.

The deliberate use of biological agents or toxins to achieve strategic military and political objectives invokes a fundamental principle not found in nature—the efforts of a thinking enemy to use biological agents to inflict death, incapacitation, or economic loss by using biological agents to confound diagnosis and frustrate treatment. The military or terrorist intent is to create conditions that are not found in nature or with natural disease epidemiology: Aerosolizing overwhelming doses of infectious agents to infect large numbers of people simultaneously with agents that are not naturally endemic and are likely to have been engineered to be more virulent than natural strains and resistant to common forms of treatment.

Conflating deliberate and natural disease threats somehow implies that by addressing the more common Mother Nature problem, the solution will be sufficient to address the deliberate biological threat. It is not. To understand this threat and confront it effectively is to understand this fundamental principle. I am afraid, we as a Nation and Government do not fully comprehend the kind of threat we are talking about today.

Fortunately, unlike cyber attacks which occur with some frequency and have received media notoriety, deliberate biological attacks have been very few and far between. It is, however, a threat that could result in enormous loss of life, severe economic losses, cause social instability, and forever change our way of life. Simply stated, biological weapons have the power to kill as many or more people as a nuclear weapon. The technological barriers to achieve this potential are significantly less than for nuclear weapons. The fact it has not happened yet may be more a matter of luck and the superb efforts of the U.S. military and intelligence community than restraint or unwillingness on the part of terrorists.

The trends emerging around the potential threat of deliberate use of biological agents are alarming. The dual-use means to cultivate, grow, and produce biological agents in quantities sufficient for nefarious use has grown smaller and more efficient, harder to locate, and diffused globally. This technology and know-how are increasingly becoming available to wider group of potential adversaries. In the past, BW was a capability reserved for nations, now it is a potential weapon for terrorist groups and disaffected individuals. Complicating this picture is the discipline of synthetic biology. The World Health Organization has assessed that advances in synthetic biology now permits adversaries to recreate pathogens no longer found in nature such as smallpox. It is conceivable in the not-too-distant future that someone could design and produce a new pathogen never seen before.

One way to consider the seriousness of the threat is to observe what Congress has said and done. Congress has mandated commissions, enacted laws, and appropriated funds going back to the late 1990's highlighting the risks from deliberate use of biological agents. In 1999, Senators Gary Hart and Warren Rudman highlighted the risk in their report entitled "A New World Coming: American Security in the 21st Century." It noted that the increase in information technology and biotechnology will cause new vulnerabilities for the United States and that the proliferation of chemical, biological, and potentially nuclear weapons that will empower and embolden both state and not-state actors to threaten or act against the United States.

In 2004, Congress passed the Project BioShield Act (Pub. L. No. 108–276) that appropriated $5.6 billion to create a guaranteed market for the acquisition of medical countermeasures against chemical, biological, radiological, and nuclear threats. An essential provision of that law was directed the Department of Homeland Security (DHS) to determine which biological threats pose a priority threat in order to prioritize medical countermeasure development and acquisition. DHS uses the Integrated Terrorism Risk Assessment findings to determine which CBRN agents present a greater risk based on the relative risk ranking against the U.S. population sufficient to affect National security. Specifically, for the highest-ranked agents, DHS evaluates the intelligence and threat information and develops and models a highly-plausible consequence scenario taking into account acquisition, production, dissemination efficacy, source strength, and meteorological conditions. This model is used to derive an estimate of the number of potentially exposed individuals at various levels of exposure, which becomes part of the Material Threat Assessment. The estimates are provided to the Department of Health and Human Services (HHS), which conducts its Public Health Consequence Modeling to determine the public health impacts.

DHS has issued about a dozen Material Threat Assessments for biological threat agents that have served as the basis for advanced development and acquisition of medical countermeasures by HHS. As mandated by law, the United States is currently researching, developing, producing, and stockpiling medical countermeasures against a variety of biological agents such as anthrax, botulinum toxin, smallpox, and other agents viewed as a credible BW or BT threat. Project BioShield funding acquires the medical countermeasures that create a powerful deterrent against this threat.

The 2008 Weapons of Mass Destruction Commission chaired by Senators Bob Graham and Jim Talent further highlighted growing trends in the spread of enabling technology and led to their principle finding that the risk of a WMD attack was rising and that the terrorist use of biological weapons was greater than the likelihood of terrorists building or obtaining a nuclear device. Their Commission recommended greater efforts to both prevent and respond to this threat. Their periodic report cards indicate that we have achieved much but still have far to go in our preparedness efforts.

The intelligence community annually reports to Congress on the threats confronting the Nation. I note that Director of National Intelligence James Clapper and other senior intelligence officials testified before the House and Senate Intelligence Committees in January of this year. Their annual assessment identifies the greatest National security threats. General Clapper stated:

"Nation-state efforts to develop or acquire weapons of mass destruction (WMD) and their delivery systems constitute a major threat to the security of the United States, deployed troops, and allies. We are focused on the threat and destabilizing effects of nuclear proliferation, proliferation of chemical and biological warfare (CBW)-related materials, and development of WMD delivery systems. The time when only a few states had access to the most dangerous technologies is past. Biological and chemical materials and technologies, almost always dual-use, move easily in the globalized economy, as do personnel with scientific expertise to design and use them. The latest discoveries in the life sciences also diffuse globally and rapidly."

He also noted note that elements of Syria's biological weapons program might have progressed beyond research and development and might have achieved limited agent production. In an environment where a variety of radical Islamic groups are fighting the Syrian government, the risk that 1 or 2 kilograms of anthrax could fall into the hands of terrorists should make us pay serious attention. During my tenure as the special assistant to the President for biodefense policy in the Bush administration, we evaluated and modeled the human and economic impact that a couple of kilograms of anthrax could have on a major metropolitan area.

The Challenge of Catastrophic Bioterrorism

Past Experience: 2001 Anthrax Attacks | Current Concern: Aerosol Release

Number that received antibiotic treatment	30,000		Number that will need antibiotic treatment	1.9-3.4 M
Number of illnesses	22		Number of illnesses	~450,000
Number of deaths	5		Number of deaths	~380,000
Decontamination	3 Buildings		Decontamination	City wide
Direct Economic Cost	>$1 B		Projected Economic Cost	>$1.8 T

In addition to Congress and the intelligence community's perspectives, I would like to offer you a more personal evaluation of the threat as it has evolved during my professional career. I come to you as an accidental tourist as it pertains to the subject of bioterrorism and biological warfare. My introduction came some 24 years ago when I was a young officer and physician assigned to the Joint Special Operations Command at Fort Bragg on the eve of the Iraqi invasion of Kuwait. I was pressed to serve as an advisor on these issues to then Major General Wayne A. Downing.

At that time, the U.S. military was marginally prepared to confront a regional power that possessed chemical and biological weapons. The military lacked the necessary protective equipment, detectors, and medical countermeasures including vaccines and antibiotics against the immediate threats posed by Iraq. Congress played a vital role in rectifying those shortfalls and our military is better prepared.

While the United States was victorious in 1991, the scale and scope of Iraq's biological weapons program remained elusive despite the most intrusive inspection and monitoring regime ever conceived and implemented by the United Nations Special Commission (UNSCOM). I experienced this first-hand, as I served as a UNSCOM biological arms inspector in 1994, 1996, and 1998. It was only after the defection of Saddam Hussein's son, Hussein Kamel, did UNSCOM and the world learn of the extent of Iraq's biological weapons. Even so, UNSCOM was never able to fully account for or verify the destruction or elimination of the biological weapons Iraq possessed or the precursors (seed stock) that were used as part of the program.

The events in Iraq and the coincident dissolution of the Former Soviet Union signified an important milestone in historical trend of biological warfare. Previous to the 1990's, biological weapons were capabilities limited to advanced nations and indeed superpowers. The defections of high-level officials from the Soviet BW program illuminated the size and sophistication of a program that involved an estimated 30,000 scientists and workers and 2 dozen large-scale facilities. The Soviets manufactured metric tons of anthrax and smallpox to be used in war with the United States. Despite the enormous scale and scope of the Soviet program, the disturbing fact is the U.S. intelligence community knew little of its existence. Once again Congress played a vital role in efforts to prevent the risk of proliferation of nuclear and biological weapons with Soviet Threat Reduction Act of 1991.

From Fort Bragg I was assigned to the Pentagon Office of the Secretary of Defense for Counter-proliferation Policy that was established after the first Gulf War. There, I witnessed the efforts to ascertain the truth behind the former Soviet Union's BW effort. The Trilateral Process between the United States, United Kingdom, and Russia stalled and the government of Russia never provided a full accounting of its BW program. The fate of these agents and associated weapons was never satisfactorily resolved. The enigma of the Russian program is only magnified when President Putin recently called for exploiting new and emerging technologies to rearm Russia and mentioned the development of genetic weapons as means "for achieving political and strategic goals."

The revelations from the Former Soviet Union and Iraq all occurred as the advances in biotechnology and molecular biology marched on in the background. The dual-use means (both the enabling technology and the know-how) continue to increase and diffuse around the globe. The means are available for any nation with modest pharmaceutical manufacturing capacity to achieve a capability with lethal equivalence to nuclear weapons.

The concern that non-state actors could divert legitimate biological process and equipment was realized when the Japanese cult Aum Shinrikyo surprised the Japanese government and the world by perpetrating a chemical nerve agent (sarin) attack in the Tokyo subway system in 1995. While the manifestation of the Aum's intentions was a nerve agent attack, Japanese law enforcement investigations uncovered Aum's efforts to develop, produce, and disseminate botulinum toxin and anthrax. The cult tried several times, fortunately unsuccessfully, to disseminate botulinum toxin and anthrax. One attempted anthrax attack targeted the U.S. naval installation at Yokohama. Probably, the greatest limitation to their effort was obtaining a virulent strain of anthrax to affect their plan. In the end they were the cult that "could not spray straight." Their incompetence was fortunate for us, but the story is not reassuring. The cult's efforts to develop both chemical and biological weapons went unnoticed by Japanese civilian authorities and U.S. intelligence agencies.

Following the attacks of September 11, I was recalled for service back into the Pentagon and was there when the initial reports about inhalational anthrax cases were first reported by the media. The National psyche after the traumatic attacks at the World Trade Center and the Pentagon was fragile and the anthrax letter attacks dealt another significant blow striking fear in every American heart about what could come next. Little did we know that the perpetrator was not al-Qaeda but a deranged scientist.

This fear, however, and the uncertainty about the identity and motives of the perpetrator(s) was enhanced when U.S. forces who invaded Afghanistan uncovered a laboratory built by al-Qaeda to research, develop, and produce anthrax (Agent X). According to the 2005 Commission on the Intelligence Capabilities of the United States Regarding Weapons of Mass Destruction:

"al-Qa'ida's biological program was further along, particularly with regard to Agent X, than pre-war intelligence indicated. The program was extensive, well-organized, and operated for two years before September 11, but intelligence insights into the program were limited. The program involved several sites in Afghanistan. Two of these sites contained commercial equipment and were operated by individuals with special training. Documents found indicated that while al-Qa'ida's primary interest was Agent X, the group had considered acquiring a variety of other biological agents. The documents obtained at the training camp included scientific articles and handwritten notes pertaining to Agent X.

"Reporting supports the hypothesis that al-Qa'ida had acquired several biological agents possibly as early as 1999, and had the necessary equipment to enable limited, basic production of Agent X. Other reporting indicates that al-Qa'ida had succeeded in isolating cultures of Agent X. Nevertheless, outstanding questions remain about the extent of biological research and development in pre-war Afghanistan, including about the reliability of the reporting described above."

The possibility that al-Qaeda then and now may still harbor the strategic intent and pursued capabilities to attack the United States with biological weapons is a lingering concern that should not be ignored.

In 2003 and 2004, I deployed to Iraq four times looking for proof of Saddam's BW program and the existence of smallpox virus cultures. It was difficult challenge under the tactical circumstances we encountered and operated in. Despite finding clandestine biological laboratories run by the Iraqi Intelligence Services, the true nature of the work and relevance to Iraq's offensive BW effort was never ascertained. Here again, despite owning the territory, apprehending and interviewing many but not all the key personalities involved, and exhaustive field investigations, the ability to uncover the truth about Iraq's BW program was never accomplished.

The limitations of intelligence were formally noted by the 2005 Commission on the Intelligence Capabilities of the United States Regarding Weapons of Mass Destruction. According to a senior CIA official interviewed for that report: "We don't know more about the biological weapons threat than we did five years ago, and five years from now we will know even less." That statement may seem astonishing but it reflects the challenge our intelligence community faces in light of the global diffusion of technology that enables practically anyone with a biology degree the means to create a biological weapon.

The risk for surprise is great. Relying entirely on intelligence assessments fails to understand the complex threat our intelligence community confronts. Understanding and preparing for the future biological threat will take more than intelligence. I highlight the vital contributing role of the National Biodefense Analysis and Countermeasure Center and two of its component entities.

- The National Bioforensic Analysis Center conducts bioforensic analysis of evidence from a biocrime or terrorist attack to attain a "biological fingerprint" to help investigators identify perpetrators and determine the origin and method of attack. It is the lead Federal facility to conduct and facilitate the technical forensic analysis and interpretation of materials recovered following a biological attack in support of the FBI.
- The National Biological Threat Characterization Center conducts studies and laboratory experiments to fill information gaps to better understand current and future biological threats; to assess vulnerabilities and conduct risk assessments; and to determine potential impacts to guide the development of countermeasures such as detectors, drugs, vaccines, and decontamination technologies.

These Centers provide critical insights and information that help the U.S. biodefense enterprise understand current and emerging threats. In the case of the anthrax letters, the forerunner to the National Bioforensic Analysis Center contributed significantly to the investigation that led to the identification of the perpetrator of those attacks. Bioforensics can play an important part in a BW deterrent strategy that links timely and accurate attribution with the credible threat of retribution to any perpetrator.

The Threat Characterization Center tests whether the hypothetical threats are real. Using valid scientific methods performing research and conducting experiments, the researchers there help bound a potential infinite risk with scientific data. They help advance the understanding of what really constitutes a threat.

I would conclude with the observation that the risk of biological attacks on the United States with biological agents is an uncertain, imminent reality. Our ability to predict or know when this threat will manifest itself is severely limited by the capabilities of our intelligence services and the wide array of potential perpetrators who could conduct such attacks. Biological weapons could inflict grievous harm on America, equal to and potentially greater than nuclear weapons, and any investments to defend against them is a modest insurance policy against an uncertain future. Our best defense remains a robust defense: A credible and rapid means to detect and mitigate such attacks and equally credible means to attribute and hold those accountable. I thank you for this opportunity and look forward to assisting you further in your efforts on this subject.

Mrs. BROOKS. Thank you.

The Chairwoman now recognizes Dr. Inglesby for 5 minutes.

STATEMENT OF TOM INGLESBY, CEO AND DIRECTOR, UPMC CENTER FOR HEALTH SECURITY

Dr. INGLESBY. Madam Chairwoman, Ranking Member Payne, Members of the subcommittee, thank you so much for the opportunity to speak to you today about bioterrorism. The Nation faces a number of major biological threats, rising levels of multi-drug anti-microbial resistance, possible pandemics of influenza, SARS, and MERS, a lab accident in which engineered pathogens could start an epidemic, but among the most serious of these facing the Nation is of course bioterrorism. My three messages for the committee today are: (1) The capability to create and use biological weapons exists widely in the world; (2) the consequences of such weapons could be major loss of life and societal disruption; and (3) while progress has been made, a great deal needs to be done to build and sustain preparedness for this threat.

The know-how to make biological weapons is now in the reach of groups or individuals with the right scientific background. Components for making biological weapons are on eBay, equipment for disseminating them is in hardware stores and agricultural supply stores. The technology is dual-use. It has both good and dangerous practical purposes in the world. It can't be locked away. There may be no obvious signal of bioweapons development, and we shouldn't expect to have warning regarding its use in the future.

The anthrax events of 2001 were shocking for the country. Letters carrying anthrax spores sickened or killed people in a number of States. Doctors were unfamiliar with the disease, major parts of Government were shut down, the source couldn't be identified. Communication from Government was very unsteady. People were afraid of their own mail. Nothing like this had happened before in our country or in any country.

It is important for this committee to know that a future biological weapons attack in the United States could look quite different from 2001 in terms of the size of attack, the form, and the numbers affected. Future events are unlikely to come with warnings that tell people to start antibiotics or get out of a building. It is more likely that the first signs of a bioterror attack will be sick people appearing in emergency rooms.

In addition, what we learn from the 1960s U.S. bioweapons program is that bioweapons don't cause normal infectious disease. As Dr. Kadlec said, they cause disease that was faster and more resistant to treatment.

A lot has been done in the last 13, 14 years to improve our preparedness for bioterrorism. In my written testimony, I have described some of things that the Federal agencies and at the State and local level are doing, some of the valuable work being done there, but there is a great deal to do going forward to make us better-prepared. Here are some of the steps I would recommend:

We need to support public health preparedness programs and medical preparedness programs through the CDC PHEP program and ASPR HPP programs. These are programs that benefit the front lines responding to bioterrorism, and they have been cut sharply in recent years. We should make good use of the new National Health Security Preparedness Index. Congress and the administration have been calling for new features of accountability, and I think this index will help along those lines in the future.

We absolutely need to sustain BioShield, BARDA, and the FDA program that we need to develop medicines and vaccines against biological threats. That process is generally working and is crucial. We need to move ahead on biosurveillance by doing a number of things. We need to set up programs that gather information from where people are getting sick in hospitals and clinics. To some extent that is going on, but we could do a better job using electronic health records that are being built across the country. We absolutely need to coordinate across Federal agencies. Critical information is being collected in a variety of Federal agencies, and it is very important to collect that and make that viewable by all.

We need to sustain well-performing laboratories. When you ask practitioners what kind of information they value the most in surveillance, they always say laboratory information because it is the most reliable. Of course, we need reliable diagnostic tools to tell us when something is going on.

Finally, we need to work together internationally. Our partners need the same protections that we do here in the United States, from pandemics, from anti-microbial resistance, and from bioterrorism, so we should work particularly hard on building this kind of global health security going forward.

Thank you again for the chance to speak to you today, and I look forward to your questions.

[The prepared statement of Dr. Inglesby follows:]

PREPARED STATEMENT OF TOM INGLESBY

FEBRUARY 11, 2014

Madame Chairwoman, Ranking Member Payne, and Members of the subcommittee, thank you for the chance to speak to you today on issues regarding the threat of bioterrorism.

My name is Tom Inglesby. I am the director and CEO of the UPMC Center for Health Security of the University of Pittsburgh Medical Center (UPMC) and associate professor of medicine and public health at the University of Pittsburgh. I'm an infectious disease physician by training.

The Center for Health Security is an independent, nonprofit organization of UPMC. Our center's mission is to protect people from the consequences of epidemics and disasters and to build resilience in communities against these challenges. My colleagues and I have been working on issues related to preparedness for bioterrorism and other major threats for the last 15 years.

There are a number of major biological threats that confront the Nation. Among these are the rising levels of antimicrobial resistance in American hospitals leading to increasing numbers of untreatable infections; the prospect of new pandemics of influenza or other novel emerging infections like SARS or MERS; the possibility of a laboratory accident in which engineered contagious pathogens cause epidemic disease; and, of course the issue prompting today's hearing, the potential for the use of biological weapons in acts of terrorism. There are many commonalities between bioterrorism and these other biological threats, and there are also aspects of the bioterrorism threat that require specific, major planning and action.

My three main messages for the committee are the following:

• The capability to create and use biological weapons exists widely in the world.
• The consequences of the use of such weapons could be substantial loss of life and societal disruption.
• While substantial progress has been made in past years, there is a great deal that needs to be done to prepare to respond to bioterrorism.

I'll elaborate on these messages in my testimony.

THE CAPABILITY TO MAKE BIOLOGICAL WEAPONS

The interest in biological weapons has been age-old in the world, as has been the capability to use them. Biological weapons have been used at various times in recorded human history at levels of sophistication consistent with the time. In ancient times, biological weapons were crude. In modern times, they became sophisticated and highly lethal. In the 1960s, the capacity to make, disseminate, test, and evaluate biological weapons was transformed. At that time, the U.S. Government funded vast programs to develop biological weapons using science and technology that was cutting-edge for those years. In those programs, they discovered how to make aerosols more stable in the environment; how to make particles float further; how to grow pathogens in high quantities; how to disseminate bacteria and viruses without inactivating them; and, much more. At the same time, other countries in the world were also studying biological weapons with their own dedicated, highly-funded programs.

In 1969, President Nixon unilaterally ended the U.S. offensive program. Then in 1972 he signed the Biological Weapons Convention saying that the United States already had enough seeds of its own destruction. That treaty led to the end of the U.S. offensive program and to the end of any country admitting it had a bioweapons development program, even though a number of countries were discovered to have had clandestine BW programs in the years since.

Now 40-some years after the signing of that treaty, the technology and know-how that was once the domain of governments, is now within reach of small groups of scientists around the world, even individual scientists with the right backgrounds. The methods for making aerosols stay airborne are widely available. The tools for making pathogens in high quantities in fermenters are on ebay. The recipes for making stable formulations of pathogens are on the internet. The equipment for disseminating these weapons is in hardware or agricultural supply stores. This information and technology is almost entirely dual-use—in the sense that it has both legitimate and dangerous uses in the world. It can't be locked away, and it wouldn't be in our interest to do so.

I understand that this committee will soon have a Classified hearing on the threat assessment. That will be important in giving you the U.S. Government assessment regarding what specific countries and groups are doing now with respect to research or development or stockpiling of biological weapons. All I will say related to this is that the workforce of scientists with microbiology and related relevant backgrounds that have enough knowledge to turn information and technology into bioweapons is countless and global. While particular threat briefings should help direct focus regarding specific terrorist groups' or countries' immediate interests in pursuing biological weapons, it is critical to understand that a country or group could change its direction on biological weapons in short order, quite possibly without any obvious signal. The former Soviet Union had a massive BW program for decades that was not visible to the outside. Given that small groups or even individuals are capable of making biological weapons and using them, we should expect not to have advanced warning regarding the development and their use.

In summary, the know-how and capability to create and use biological weapons exists widely in the world. This will only grow with time as the tools and techniques of biotechnology become more broadly disseminated, less expensive, and valuable to growing economies globally.

THE CONSEQUENCES OF BIOLOGICAL WEAPONS

The anthrax events of 2001 were shocking for the country. Letters carrying anthrax spores were sent to a number of people in different cities. Hospitals, doctors, and nurses at the time were largely unfamiliar with the disease. Elements of all three branches of Government were each affected and closed at some point. Buildings had to be evacuated for prolonged periods. Cases appeared over weeks in different places. A number of people were sickened and killed. The source of the anthrax could not be identified. The communication about it from our own Government was often uncertain and changing. The media coverage was constant. People were afraid of their own mail. Nothing like this had happened before in our country or any country.

A great deal has been done to improve our ability to recognize and respond to biological weapons events since that time. I will say more about that below. But it is important for this committee to know that a future biological weapons attack on the United States could look quite different that the 2001 anthrax incident—in terms of size of attack, form, and the numbers affected.

The anthrax letters of 2001 came with a warning in them, which allowed some people to begin taking protective antibiotics and initiate evacuation. Future events are unlikely to come with warnings like that. It is more likely that the first sign of a bioterror attack will be sick people appearing in clinics and emergency rooms. And while the anthrax letters of 2001 came through the mail, future bioterrorism attacks could come in many different kinds of form. There are many means of creating aerosols. And there are clearly other means of using biological weapons against the public.

We also need to understand that the scope of future bioweapons events could be far, far greater that what we saw in 2001. In 2009, the U.S. National Security Council said: "The effective dissemination of a lethal biological agent within an unprotected population could place at risk the lives of hundreds of thousands of people. The unmitigated consequences of such an event could overwhelm our public health capabilities, potentially causing an untold number of deaths. The economic cost could exceed $1 trillion for each such incident." The use of such weapons could lead to substantial loss of life and great societal disruption. Even with a small or modest-sized attack, the social and economic impact would be significant.

BUILD OUR ABILITY TO RESPOND

In the last 10 years, progress in preparedness has been made in a number of areas. There are now a cadre of Government officials, public health experts, doctors, nurses, and scientists who have become knowledgeable and skilled in thinking through and planning for biological terrorism. That community of experts in and out of Government didn't exist in 2001. There are also a series of major biopreparedness programs across the U.S. Government, some of which I will cite here. HHS/ASPR has funded hospital preparedness programs around the country and runs valuable programs like the National Disaster Medical System. NIH has a basic research program for biodefense. BARDA has developed a number of medications and vaccines that could be critical in future bio responses. CDC has funded State and local public health agencies to prepare for bioterrorism (among other crises and disasters) and it oversees laboratory research in this area, manages a strategic National stockpile of medications for use in an emergency, and has an Emergency Operations Center that is a model for other health agencies around the world. DHS has created a risk assessment and threat characterization process to help guide planning. FDA has created an office that deals explicitly with the regulation and approval of products only to be used in the event of bioterrorism, pandemics, or other urgencies or emergencies. The DOD and DOS have important programs dedicated to addressing the issue overseas through science and technology as well as cooperative threat reduction. Taken together, these efforts, combined with the substantial hard work of State and local public health agencies, hospitals, emergency management and civic organizations, have put the country on a better footing in its ability to respond to major biothreats.

Our Center's 2013 study of the U.S. Federal biodefense funding found that 90 percent of the biodefense budget served additional purposes beyond biodefense. The good news in that number is that these additional purposes are valuable such as public health agency preparedness for disasters, hospital planning for crises, and research that improves our response to infectious diseases. The down side of that 90 percent number is that there has been an inflated sense of what is actually been spent on biodefense; that effort is not nearly as big as it looks at first pass.

The more work that is done in this field, the more it becomes clear what we still need to prepare for to respond to bioterrorism and to sustain the preparations that have been made to date. What follows are my recommendations for what we need to pay particular attention to in the years ahead in terms of biopreparedness.

STRENGTHEN MEDICAL AND PUBLIC HEALTH PREPAREDNESS

In the event of bioterrorism, the people who would be on the front lines responding are largely comprised of public health, medical, and hospital professionals. They will be the ones most likely to discover that something has gone wrong and to initiate laboratory testing for what is behind it. They are the ones who will be called to rapidly investigate what is happening, and where and how the bioterrorism occurred. Following an act of bioterrorism, there may be no announcement, and there is likely to be no "site" that can be cordoned off—just sick people appearing in emergency rooms and clinics. Public health and medical leaders will be asked to advise our political leaders on the right course of action for administering prophylactic care to prevent illness, for treating those who are sick, for identifying those at greatest risk of falling ill. And they will be the ones who are providing medical care within hospitals.

Given the importance to bioterrorism preparedness of these professionals and the agencies and institutions in which they work, their work needs to be supported. Funding for the public health emergency preparedness program (PHEP), which funds State and local health agencies to prepare for bioterrorism and other disasters, has been cut by more than $100 million in the last 5 years. In addition, funding support for the National hospital preparedness program fell 33% last year, and is down nearly 50% from its inception. I'm really concerned about these reductions and trends, and how this sharp decline in funding will weaken these programs. In fact, we are already seeing a dramatic reduction in total per capita funding for emergency preparedness in the States, which will inevitably results in a reduction in our capability to respond when emergencies strike.

It is worth calling your attention to the National Health Security Preparedness Index that was launched in December by 20 collaborating organizations. This is a first-of-its-kind index that has as its purpose the measurement of the level of National and State health security preparedness. It uses 128 indicators that gauge State capacities and capabilities in the domains of health surveillance, incident and information management, countermeasure management, community planning and engagement, and surge management. Based on those indicators, scores are calculated that State and local preparedness communities and National policy makers can use to judge how well prepared we are, and how to continue to strengthen the collective efforts. The overall score for the country in December was 7.2 out of 10, with varying results in the States around the country. This score shows that we have built some capacity in a number of realms. But it also makes clear how much more we need to do. To make these scores improve will require focus and more resources. If, on the other hand, resources for these key National programs continue to slide, then I am concerned that index scores in the coming years will decline. We shouldn't let that happen.

Another critical element of our public health and medical preparedness is the development of medicines and vaccines for use following a biological attack. Development of these products is a complex, sometimes decade-long process with inherent risks of failure, as is the case with drug and vaccine development more broadly. It is difficult to persuade the major pharmaceutical companies to engage in this effort because of the uncertainties of Government policy and action, and because of the opportunity costs associated with doing this work as opposed to other more economically-valuable opportunities. A variety of programs and policies have been established over the years to try to deal with this challenge. Earlier critical steps to deal with this were the creation of the BioShield fund and the establishment of the BARDA advanced research and development program. The loss of the multi-year BioShield fund has been a setback for the USG effort to develop countermeasures. It creates new uncertainty for the private sector. The single-year BioShield appropriation for fiscal year 2014 is about equivalent to half of what had been available annually in years prior.

On the other hand, there has been a positive change in the way BARDA is now funded. In past years, advanced development at BARDA had been funded by diverting BioShield funds, which was not how the funds were intended. Fiscal year 2014 is the first year since fiscal year 2008 that BARDA advanced research and development has received funds from Congress directly and not from BioShield. It is important that BARDA continue to receive appropriations that are separate and distinct from BioShield. The purposes of BioShield and BARDA are distinct and should be funded accordingly.

Another major contributor to success in the program to develop countermeasures is the FDA program, established explicitly to support the regulatory process for these medicines and vaccines. This has been a highly successful program and should continue to get strong support.

It is worth underscoring again in the context of countermeasure development that we really need to come to grips with what was learned in the bioweapons programs from the 1960s. From those programs we learned that some biological weapons did not cause illness in the same patterns as naturally-occurring infectious diseases. Among other things, they caused illness on an accelerated time course, and they had the ability to overwhelm traditional treatment strategies. As we continue to improve and build our countermeasure development efforts and broader planning efforts, we need to make sure our planning for today takes into account what we learned from those earlier years.

MAKE WISE INVESTMENTS IN BIOSURVEILLANCE

The U.S. Government definition of biosurveillance comes from Homeland Security Presidential Directive 21. There it is defined as "the process of active data-gathering with appropriate analysis and interpretation of biosphere data that might relate to disease activity and threats to human or animal health—whether infectious, toxic, metabolic, or otherwise, and regardless of intentional or natural origin—in order to achieve early warning of health threats, early detection of health events, and overall situational awareness of disease activity."

We need biosurveillance systems to help us detect and understand new outbreaks and to discover specific signals related to bioterrorism or other health events. There are many information needs that would immediately and urgently arise following an act of bioterrorism: How many people are sick? By what means is the disease spreading? What are the risk factors and how do we control them? What public health interventions are working? Are treatments working safely and effectively? And many other related questions. We need systems that can answers these questions.

To do this requires good information systems, analytic capability and health expertise. At the Federal level, that means sharing information across the agencies quickly. Information that can bear directly on outbreak discovery and control can come from public health, the agricultural sector, commerce, private industry, overseas disease surveillance networks, and many other channels. Programs like NBIC that are intended to share and organize that information across Federal agencies and with State and local partners are critical. We should also support innovation and research into whether we can use social media and mobile technologies to identify outbreaks early.

At the local level, public health leaders also need information systems that give them insight into what is happening within hospitals during outbreaks. This requires collaboration between medical institutions and public health agencies in ways that helps them identify new patterns of disease in outbreaks, and gauges the effectiveness and safety of medicines and vaccines in automated, rapid fashion.

Disease surveillance also requires good laboratory diagnostics. When you ask public health officials what kind of surveillance information they place highest value on, they consistently tell you that laboratory data is the most prized because it provides definitive diagnosis of an illness or an outbreak. Laboratory diagnoses of serious infectious diseases that are made in a clinic or a hospital are not always automatically transmitted to public health officials who would be responsible for communicating about them to the public and to political leaders. We also need to continue to push ahead to develop rapid diagnostic tests for bioterrorism-related and other infectious diseases, recognizing that there is no commercial market for these products, so they will need continued Government development support and Government purchase.

A few words on environmental surveillance. I understand you will be holding a future hearing on this issue. So I will only comment here to say that there is a clear need for environmental surveillance, but it has to work in the real-world situation where it will reside. If State and local public health agencies are to be part of the system (and they have expertise and tools that are needed for these systems to work), then they need to understand and believe in the value and the effectiveness of these systems. If State and local leaders don't have the confidence to take action following an environmental surveillance alarm when it goes off, then that is not a well-functioning system. So in addition to all the development, testing, and evaluation of these environmental systems, a continued examination and testing of how they are actually working in places around the country is critical.

IMPROVE GLOBAL HEALTH SECURITY

The work we need to do to prepare for bioterrorism has much in common with the work we need to do to respond to pandemic influenza, emerging infectious diseases, and antimicrobial resistance, particularly as we work with our international partners around the world on these challenges.

Each of these problems requires a workforce that knows how to recognize new outbreaks and new patterns of infectious disease. Each of them depends on scientific research to improve our understanding. Each of these issues could cause serious response challenges in the medical and public health communities. And in each of these realms, we have to cope with the reality that markets themselves have not been enough to create the new medicines, vaccines, and diagnostics that are needed. The required preparations and responses to these issues are the same for our international partners as they are for us. It is important to see the ways in which working together on them makes sense and can create valuable synergy.

In conclusion, there has been consistent progress in recent years in our efforts to prepare for bioterrorism and related threats. But there remains a great deal of critical work to be done. Over the last decade, we have witnessed a slow but steady decline in attention to bioterrorism preparedness issues, in part because we haven't experienced another bioterror attack since 2001. But we have no reason—from a technical perspective or consequence management perspective—to let our guard down. I thank you for holding this hearing to address these issues. The efforts of this committee as well as other efforts in Congress can help to ensure we make continued forward progress in areas of great National importance in preparing for bioterrorism.

Mrs. BROOKS. Thank you, Dr. Inglesby.
The Chairwoman now recognizes Dr. Cole for 5 minutes.

STATEMENT OF LEONARD A. COLE, DIRECTOR, TERROR MEDICINE AND SECURITY, DEPARTMENT OF EMERGENCY MEDICINE, RUTGERS NEW JERSEY MEDICAL SCHOOL

Dr. COLE. Thank you. Chairwoman Brooks, Ranking Member Payne, distinguished Members of this subcommittee, and of the larger and full Homeland Security Committee, thank you for inviting me to speak on the threat posed by bioterrorism to the American homeland and elsewhere. I am grateful as well to the full committee's Chairman McCaul and Ranking Member Thompson for their leadership on Homeland Security. Since I see he has come back, I must also recognize the Congressman who, on many—for many reasons I have huge regard for, and in the neighboring county—represents people in the neighboring county to the one I live in, so we need you on our side.

In 2012, and again last year, I was privileged to address the Subcommittee on Counterterrorism and Intelligence during which I referenced the 2012 paper titled, "WMD Terrorism." The paper was produced by the Aspen Institute's Homeland Security WMD Working Group of which I was a member. One of the paper's conclusions, still valid, is that bioterrorism remains a continuing and serious threat.

In the wake of last April's Boston Marathon bombings, Ricin-laced letters were mailed to several public officials, including one to President Obama. Just last week, Israel's Supreme Court upheld an indictment against a detained Palestinian operative for al-Qaeda who was charged with developing biological weapons under the direction of the organization's leader, Ayman al-Zawahiri.

Since the anthrax attacks in 2001, the U.S. Government has spent more than $60 billion on biosecurity programs. They range from enhancing methods of disease detection to developing more effective antibiotics, vaccines, and other countermeasures.

Despite progress in the Nation's preparedness and response capabilities, deficiencies remain. I cite three here that I think warrant particular attention. The first is the need for expanded education and training throughout the medical community. The level of preparedness for a biological assault varies from one location to another. Where drills are conducted frequently and in realistic settings, optimal outcomes are more likely. The effective medical response at the Boston bombings was credited not only to the availability of excellent personnel and hospitals, but to the high quality of pre-event drills.

These exercises included mock biological attacks. In many locations, budget pressures and human inertia have resulted in cutbacks in the frequency and quality of exercises. Failure to maintain proper levels of education and training diminishes the likelihood of a successful medical outcome at an actual incident.

A second area of concern relates to the special needs of children, and I reference as well the concerns of Representative Payne, Ranking Member Payne on this issue, the special needs of children during a biological attack. Children are particularly vulnerable to biological agents because of their more rapid respiratory rate, greater skin permeability, and lower fluid reserve than that of adults, yet medical response plans typically are adult-specific and do not include allowances for these differences. Compounding this concern, a 2013 article cited studies showing that most physicians feel unprepared to address a bioterrorism attack. These studies included a survey of Michigan pediatricians who were deemed "overwhelmingly underprepared to deal with an event."

The third issue that deserves particular attention is the need for legislation that directly addresses the threat of biological and other weapons of mass destruction. I understand that Representatives Pascrell and King are reintroducing the WMD Preparedness and Response Act. Although previous incarnations of the bill have drawn unanimous endorsement from the House Committee on Homeland Security, it is not yet law. Regarding the biothreat, the act would heighten laboratory security, help create uniform standards for handling dangerous biological agents, and support appointment of a special assistant to the President to coordinate biodefense policy. The proponents of this bill deserve high praise, and I wish them every success toward its enactment.

In concluding, I note that it is no more possible to completely eliminate bioterrorism than it is to completely eliminate infectious disease. Still, enhancing security measures reduces the portals of opportunity for a would-be perpetrator. Further making biological terrorism more difficult to actuate is bound to discourage individuals and groups from even trying. Diminishing the threat is surely a worthy goal shared by people of good will everywhere. Thank you.

[The prepared statement of Dr. Cole follows:]

PREPARED STATEMENT OF LEONARD A. COLE [1]

FEBRUARY 11, 2014

Chairman Brooks, Ranking Member Payne, distinguished Members of this subcommittee, thank you for inviting me to speak on the threat posed by bioterrorism to the American homeland and elsewhere. I am grateful as well to the full committee's Chairman McCaul and Ranking Member Thompson for their leadership on homeland security. In 2012 and again last year, I was privileged to address the Subcommittee on Counterterrorism and Intelligence during which I referenced a 2012 paper titled *WMD Terrorism*. The paper was produced by the Aspen Institute's Homeland Security WMD Working Group, of which I was a member. One of the paper's conclusions, still valid, is that bioterrorism remains a continuing and serious threat.

Pathogenic microorganisms and toxins such as anthrax bacteria or botulinum toxin are relatively easy to acquire and grow. Disseminating anthrax can be as simple as sending dried spores through the U.S. mail, which is exactly what happened in the weeks following the 9/11 attacks. About half-a-dozen anthrax letters infected at least 22 people, 5 of whom died. Spores were later found to have leaked from the letters during mail processing and delivery. As a result, scores of buildings including U.S. House and Senate office buildings had become contaminated and were shut down—some for several years. More than 30,000 people at risk of exposure received prophylactic antibiotic treatment.

The bio-threat continues. In the wake of last April's Boston Marathon bombings, ricin-laced letters were mailed to several public officials, including one to President Obama. Just last week, Israel's Supreme Court upheld an indictment against a detained Palestinian operative for al-Qaeda, who was charged with developing biological weapons under direction of the organization's leader, Ayman al-Zawahiri.

Since bacteria and viruses reproduce and multiply, unlike any other weapon they can make an environment more dangerous with the passage of time. If resistant to medical countermeasures they could kill many thousands. Yet much can be done to minimize this risk. Since the anthrax attacks in 2001, the U.S. Government has spent more than $60 billion on biosecurity programs. They range from enhancing methods of disease detection to developing more effective antibiotics, vaccines, and other countermeasures. Despite progress in the Nation's preparedness and response capabilities, deficiencies remain. I cite three here that I think warrant particular attention.

The first is the need for expanded education and training throughout the medical community.[2] The level of preparedness for a biological assault varies from one location to another. Where drills are conducted frequently and in realistic settings, optimal outcomes are more likely. The effective medical response at the Boston bombings was credited not only to the availability of excellent personnel and hospitals but to the high quality of pre-event drills. Those exercises included mock biological attacks.

In many locations budget pressures and human inertia have resulted in cutbacks in the frequency and quality of exercises. Failure to maintain proper levels of edu-

---

[1] Unless otherwise indicated the views expressed here are my own and not representative of any institution.

[2] A course on Terror Medicine is being taught this semester at Rutgers New Jersey Medical School, to my knowledge the first such course at an American medical school.

cation and training diminishes the likelihood of a successful medical outcome at an actual incident.

A second area of concern relates to the special needs of children during a biological attack. On its website, the American Academy of Pediatrics notes that children are particularly vulnerable to biological agents because of their more rapid respiratory rate, greater skin permeability, and lower fluid reserve than that of adults. Yet medical response plans typically are adult-specific and do not include allowances for these differences.

Children comprise 23 percent of the population. Making a diagnosis in this group can be complicated especially among the very young who are unable to describe their symptoms or discuss how they might have been exposed.

Compounding this concern, a 2013 article cited studies showing that most physicians feel unprepared to address a bioterrorism attack. The studies included a survey of Michigan pediatricians, 85 percent of whom had never participated in a bioterrorism training exercise. The authors of the survey concluded that these pediatricians were "overwhelmingly underprepared to deal with an event."[3]

The third issue that deserves particular attention is the need for legislation that directly addresses the threat of biological and other weapons of mass destruction. I understand that Representatives Pascrell and King are reintroducing the WMD Preparedness and Response Act, versions of which they have sponsored in the past. Although previous incarnations of the bill have drawn unanimous endorsement from the House Committee on Homeland Security Committee, it is not yet law.

In 2008 the bipartisan WMD Commission called for measures now part of the bill including the establishment of a National strategy to counter the threat of weapons of mass destruction. Regarding the bio-threat, the act would heighten laboratory security, help create uniform standards for handling dangerous biological agents, and support appointment of a special assistant to the President to coordinate biodefense policy. The proponents of this bill deserve high praise, and I wish them every success toward its enactment.

In concluding I note that it is no more possible to completely eliminate bioterrorism as a threat than to completely eliminate infectious disease. Still, enhancing security measures reduces the portals of opportunity for a would-be perpetrator. Further, making biological terrorism more difficult to actuate is bound to discourage individuals and groups from even trying. Diminishing the threat is surely a worthy goal shared by people of good will everywhere.

Mrs. BROOKS. Thank you, Dr. Cole.

At this time, the Chairwoman is now just pleased to recognize Congressman Pascrell, and so pleased that you could be here because of your extensive work on this issue, and so we appreciate you taking time out of your calendar to make sure you can be here today. As much time as you may consume.

Mr. PASCRELL. Madam Chairwoman, it is an honor to be here, and with our Ranking Member, and it is good to hear the experts that you have called and assembled here. I am very, very familiar with Dr. Cole, and we have been at this a long time, at least it seems a long time anyway.

We have to go back to 9/11 reports to the Congress of the United States, and this is the one area, Madam Chairwoman, this is the one area that we have been absolutely negligent. We have not done near enough to address the issues which the 9/11 Commission laid before us. I articulated it to the "nth" degree.

As a Member, original Member of the Homeland Security, we tried to do our best to implement the recommendations of the 9/11 Commission. They weren't all implemented immediately, as we well know. This has a long, long history, unfortunately, but I

---

[3] Following are links to references about preparedness and the vulnerability of children to a biological attack: *http://journals.lww.com/smajournalonline/Fulltext/2013/01000/Preparedness_of_Rural_Physicians_for_Bioterrorist.7.aspx*; *http://www.aap.org/en-us/advocacy-and-policy/aap-health-initiatives/Children-and-Disasters/Pages/Biological-Terrorism-and-Agents.aspx*; *http://globalbiodefense.com/2013/02/05/bioterrorism-preparedness-the-forgotten-patient-population/#sthash.X9whD34M.dpuf*; *http://www.ncbi.nlm.nih.gov/pubmed/19194343*.

don't sense, Madam Chairwoman, the urgency about this, and I think our three—I did read Dr. Inglesby's testimony, they have all basically said the same thing, too, about that issue. Why isn't it that we are not addressing it? I mean, we spent over $60 billion, and so like a lot of money we spent in Homeland Security that went for naught because if we don't have a coordination of agencies, then nothing is going to work. This is serious business, regardless of which part of this, you know, we are talking about. So I want to thank you and Ranking Member Payne for allowing me to say a few words today.

We are going to reintroduce, Peter King and myself, the Weapons of Mass Destruction Preparedness and Prevention Act today. For the past three Congresses, I worked with Mr. King to enact this much-needed legislation, to establish comprehensive protection and response in addressing a threat of weapons of mass destruction. This wide-ranging bill addresses all aspects of our preparedness frame-working. It touches upon prevention, protection. Prevention, you have heard our witnesses talk about education, tremendously lacking, directed only to one subgroup and not to the entire population, particularly to our kids; the protection of our population and what responses we have, God forbid, when any—whether it is chemical, biological, radiological, or nuclear attacks occur, what do we do? Are we prepared? You have heard what our witnesses said.

So, we have a long way to go. Then finally, recovery. How do we recover from such a dastardly situation? Are we prepared to recover? We live in a very important and critical age. It has brought us some terrible things, but it is also hope for the future that not only we can prevent these things—and it is never going to be seamless, we know that. I am glad you are bold enough and brave enough to say that. Most relevant, I think, to the topic to today's discussion, this legislation requires a new top-down strategy from the White House for a better intergovernmental approach, meeting the need for Nation-wide monitoring of biological threats. That is, I think, very paramount to our efforts. We may—we need to make this issue a priority.

Remember, we created the Talent/Graham Weapons of Mass Destruction Commission because of the extreme gravity of this threat, particularly from a biological attack. Madam Chairwoman, that is a long time ago we did that. After 12 years, we still do not have a comprehensive strategy. Versions of the WMD Prevention and Preparedness Act have passed out of this committee twice, but unfortunately, it never made it to the floor.

When you guys were the Majority, when we guys were, so I mean, there is enough concern around here to go around. Meanwhile, there does not appear to be any momentum in this administration to tackle the pressing issue of terrorism, bioterrorism. I was encouraged to see that the White House released the National Strategy on Biosurveillance in July 2012. It fell short on substance. The strategy was far from what Congressman King and I envisioned in the WMD bill. I hoped—I had hoped that the implementation plan, which was supposed to be released by December 2012 would fill the gaps. It still hasn't been released. That is totally unacceptable. I mean, this is either a priority or it is not, and when everything is a priority, nothing is a priority.

I am pleased that Mr. King has agreed to work with me on this by introducing the measure today. I think this is a matter of life and death. It has been over 2 years since the WMD Center, the successor to the WMD Commission released its "Bio-Response Report Card." You look at that report card, and you have to wonder, and it would scare legislators, so think about what it will do the public. It has been made public. I don't know if anybody ever read the darn thing.

In the absence of progress on robust legislative initiatives, such as this bipartisan bill, little has changed. Doctor, can I just ask Dr. Cole?

Mrs. BROOKS. Absolutely.

Mr. PASCRELL. Dr. Cole, I am highly concerned, as all three of you are, with the continued lack of progress in our preparedness. The WMD Prevention and Preparedness Act calls for a comprehensive strategy across the entire Federal Government to counter bio threats. What is the current level of coordination between agencies on these issues as you see it and how do you believe we can improve it? Because I think that is at the core of us moving and getting out of our quicksand here.

Dr. COLE. I wish I had a very good answer for this. I do not. In part, I am not part of the Governmental apparatus and the day-to-day affairs of interagency cooperation. I am aware of several initiatives that are being directed at this problem, certainly in the Health and Human Services Department and advances in Bio-Shield in particular. I don't know how one can raise the level of consciousness to an appropriate degree. A lot of this is psychological. We can all imagine, God forbid that it should happen, that if there were a major biological incident in the next week, 1 minute after the word got out that this was the case, there would be attention around the country and would be again revved up.

My short answer has to be that holding hearings like this with prominent spokespersons reminding everybody of the importance of this issue can only be to the good. As I said in any remarks, I think it is terrific that you and Representative King are going to be reintroducing the WMD bill.

Mr. PASCRELL. Well, we are not going to be discouraged. You know, we don't give up. We are not smart enough to give up. Would either two gentleman like to jump in and briefly respond to that? I would appreciate it.

Dr. KADLEC. Well, I may have a little more insight than Dr. Cole other than to say that it really does take some leadership at the very top to basically drive this problem. In my experience, and I had the title, was basically, you know, working the issue 24/7, 365. I think that is really what it takes, and it basically is more than just an individual. It takes, you know, literally the President to make this a priority. I will just highlight his making the nuclear terrorism issue a priority has made a difference, has mobilized not only the world, but the U.S. Government to work against that problem, and clearly this is a similar nature that requires the same kind of attention and commitment, too.

Mr. PASCRELL. Dr. Inglesby.

Dr. INGLESBY. I agree. Well, I think the first dilemma for all of us is that the functions of biodefense are really going to have to reside in different agencies. It is very hard to imagine at an implementation-level point that we gather because HHS has to do certain things, CDC has to do certain things, DOD, et cetera, so there is going to be challenge for coordination, so it is really important what you pointed out. I think the people actually leading those programs, their personalities and their ability to stay on the issue is really fundamental. I think we do both when Bob was in office and now, I think there are a lot of very impressive people running those programs, but obviously we could always get—we need to improve coordination.

Mr. PASCRELL. Madam—Thank you. Madam Chairwoman, I don't know if we have to work backwards for folks to understand how devastating any of these attacks could be on a small level and a large level. We—we need to get—make sure that there is a sense of urgency on this administration and future administrations about this very critical issue, and I applaud you for what you are doing, both of you, in order to get this in front of the public again, because if we don't address it, we saw what happened on what we would consider to be, relatively speaking, smaller attacks.

I mean, when you—when you look at what could happen in what we call "Oil Alley," the New Jersey Turnpike up in through the Elizabeth area, which is—FBI has called probably the most dangerous area in the entire country, I mean, you have a catastrophic incident there, you will put immediately 1.5 million people in jeopardy. I don't know how better to say it. I mean, if that doesn't make you think about what the heck we are doing, nothing will. Our bill won't, discussions won't, this is serious business, and I thank you for your work.

Mrs. BROOKS. Well, I thank you, Congressman Pascrell, for your leadership, for you and Congressman King continuing to fight this battle Congress after Congress, and I assure you that this committee and—will continue to fight the battle as well. Thank you for pointing out the Bio-Response Report Card, which while it was in our materials, it shows—and while we are all used to A through F grades, there are no As on this report card. There are a lot of Fs on the report card, a lot of Ds, such as medical countermeasure development and approval process, such as medical countermeasure availability, and medical management, all of the things that our witnesses have talked about, and so it is—it is clear that we are not yet prepared and that we have a long way to go, even though there have been, you know folks like yourselves working on this for quite sometime.

So, we appreciate, we look forward to working with you on movement of your bill and with hopeful passage and very much appreciate your leadership in this Congress. Thank you.

At this time, I will recognize myself for 5 minutes of questioning, and I want to build a bit on some of the points that have already been made. Again, talking a bit about the coordination. Because there is no leadership, a biodefense advisor as you were, Dr. Kadlec, to President Bush, there is, at this time, not a person singularly responsible for this.

The GAO testified before the subcommittee in April 2011 that development of medical countermeasures for biological and other threats is a complicated business, and as I just brought up with this biodefense report card, we are really not doing well on that—on that measure. The business starts with a declaration by Department of Homeland Security that a virus or bacteria or chemical or other agent is a material threat. It then becomes incumbent, as you said, Dr. Inglesby, upon HHS to work with industry to develop pharmaceuticals that can help meet the threat. GAO has reported that the coordination between DHS and HHS has not been optimal and could benefit from clarification between the two agencies on time frames, milestones, and written procedures.

This is a question for the entire panel: How do you think these agencies are working? What should we be doing to encourage or require DHS to be doing to facilitate the smooth transition of threat information to HHS to assist with this counterdevelopment, development process? Because, as we have seen from this report card, we are simply not prepared.

So, I would like to start out with you, Dr. Kadlec, and then each of the panel to talk about our preparedness and the coordination between those agencies, and working also with industry.

Dr. KADLEC. Certainly. There exists within the enterprise, if you will, this Public Health Emergency Medical Countermeasures Enterprise, PHEMCE, which is really a way to convene the interagency group at levels below the White House levels. While I think that is effective in terms of what is a polite coordination, the question is, is whether or not the priorities that have been outlined by DHS have been effectively acted upon by HHS, and quite frankly, that is not a polite conversation that has to happen, and clearly, I think, has to go a level above.

To think about how you could effectively maybe encourage, or coerce better coordination, you have the report card that you identify doesn't get into details that have been identified, but I do know that there have been 12 agents on them, material threat determinations have been made, and it may be helpful to have a report card issued each year that looks at the progress against those 12 different agents. I through you would find that probably you will find some real progress in one area, or maybe two, but not much progress in other areas.

So I think the question is, is I think that is one way to monitor this effort. I do believe that in some ways the role of the White House reigns supreme here, and while we are fixated on the idea of a senior leader in that position, I also think that one of the important roles of the Government is really with the Office of Management and Budget, and they were our greatest ally to basically have these kinds of conversations with the interagency, subject to the progress or nonprogress that has been made.

So I think in some ways it really does require good oversight by Congress, and certainly transparency in terms of the progress that is being obtained, as well as leaders inside and outside the process to ensure that it is met.

Mrs. BROOKS. Thank you for those suggestions. Dr. Inglesby.

Dr. INGLESBY. Yes, this is a really complicated process, and I think it has been evolving—I am sorry. Thank you. It is a very complicated process. It has been evolving, I think, in the right direction, albeit not as fast as we would like over the years. I think that my sense from the outside is that DHS and HHS are communicating better about the risk assessment process than before.

I don't know that the risk assessment process is what is rate limiting right now as much as is resource and decisions, terrible decisions that have to be made between do we develop this versus this versus this. At some point, I think the whole process run into a resource dilemma. If you took what they are being asked to do and gave it to the private sector, the private sector developing its own medicines and vaccines could not do in terms of resource what we have asked the Government to do, to make new medicines and vaccines.

So I think overall there is a resource limitation. I do think, at Bob's idea of looking at what of the 12 things that are material threat determinations, how much progress we have made on those, always thinking about whether or not we need to elevate something new as a new material threat. I think that is a very logical way to go, and we have much further to go on all those things, but my sense is that, in the end, that is largely what we are able to make available, given budget austerity.

Mrs. BROOKS. Thank you very much. Dr. Cole.

Dr. COLE. The situation, as I hear it being discussed, and I have thought about it myself, reminds me of the dilemma that was posed some years back, not too many years ago, before there was a Director of National Intelligence. There was not one single person with an authority even to convene the various intelligence agencies.

Now, the 16 or so intelligence agencies are part of an umbrella that is directed by an individual, a capable individual, we always hope to be capable, and I would think that same importance should be applied to this. Now, Bob Kadlec made some remarks, and I think perhaps he is being overly modest, but he can refer to his own experience about the advantage not only of having a single coordinator, but one who is stationed in the White House and therefore draws the prestige of the Presidency in the White House when he or she were to call meetings to gather together to come to some kind of coordinated and coherent policy.

Mrs. BROOKS. Thank you very much. I now recognize Ranking Member Mr. Payne from New Jersey for questions.

Mr. PAYNE. Thank you, Madam Chairwoman.

Dr. Cole, as I indicated in my opening statement, I am concerned about the 40 percent of countermeasures in the Strategic National Stockpile are not approved for children. That gives me great reason for pause, and what are our greatest challenges to developing countermeasures for children?

Dr. COLE. Well, I think this relates to some of what I referred to before as raising the issue of concern in appropriate quarters. I would be happy to think of the White House having a coordinator who could then underscore the importance of the filling some other gaps as well, but particularly this one as it applies to children, and which you so appropriately made reference to.

Now, this is not just your or my concern. The various pediatric associations, I believe it is the American Academy of Pediatrics has made a very clear concern about this. In terms of how this would be approached in the National Strategic Stockpile, that would be just one element in terms of helping to prepare better defenses and responses on behalf of children, and that would include, as I referenced, medical training, appropriate individuals being informed, local public health authorities, right through what is placed into our stockpile for defenses.

Mr. PAYNE. Dr. Inglesby.

Dr. INGLESBY. Well, I certainly agree with your judgment that we need to do more for the pediatric population. I think Dr. Cole's comments are very logical and sensible. I think part of that education comes from what HHS is trying to do with hospitals in the hospital preparedness program and what we are doing to prepare kids—prepare for kids' illnesses and injuries at the hospital level. I do think the countermeasure development program needs to much more carefully incorporate pediatric needs. The dilemmas are not just financial there, but they are ethical. I know that you-all know very well how difficult it is to develop a medicine for a child that would only be used in the event of a National emergency.

I mean, the ethics systems that we have now require us to only test medicines in kids when they can have a direct benefit and—so, it poses a new and very difficult problem that the President's Bioethics Commission took on very well. That doesn't get us out of having to spend much more thought and time and resource on the problem, so I do agree with you and think we should.

Mr. PAYNE. Dr. Kadlec.

Dr. KADLEC. Sir, I would just endorse the comments made by Dr. Cole and Dr. Inglesby. I do believe the ethical issues are certainly significant and no trivial matter. I do believe there is an element of priority though, and focus on this to understand that in some ways we have a very significant obligation to those most vulnerable in our society to protect them, and I think in some ways that is a reminder that needs to pervade the whole effort, whether it be the policies, whether it be the programmatics, the advanced development, the procurements, as well as the FDA testing that goes around this to ensure that we do keep an eye to that problem.

It is not an easy problem and certainly one that would benefit from some more resources, but I do believe more attention, and, as you pointed out, sir, very eloquently, the realization that we have this very significant obligation to these children.

Mr. PAYNE. Okay. I would just like to ask each one of you: How can Government in our part and industry efforts improve to better protect our children?

I hear the ethical issue, which seems like it is probably pretty difficult to get around that. But what can we do to work with industry to protect our children from these dangerous bioagents?

Dr. KADLEC. Well, I will just give you a tangible one. I think, in terms of the annual—or the—they are not frequent, but I think the notion that the frequent requests for proposals that come from the Government—I can't recall one that specifically calls out the children in any form or fashion. It would seem to me that would be an appropriate thing to do, to identify particular products or product preparations that would be more amenable for children.

I just note that in some ways some antibiotics that we have in the Strategic National Stockpile are not formulated in a way that would be easy to give to the children—for either the parents to give or the children to accept. So I think that is one little example of what you could do practically to address that.

Mr. PAYNE. So be more specific in the RFP.

Dr. KADLEC. As well as have specific RFPs for pediatric preparations.

Dr. INGLESBY. I think that is a good idea. I think maybe another thing to consider is whether or not we should be more explicit in our requirement-setting process.

Because the Government really is driven by requirements and, if we formally establish in some way some requirement for pediatric formulations, then that would drive work and direction.

I am not sure I have a proposal on how to do that. But to the extent that it is not happening now, we should consider doing that.

Dr. COLE. I have the strange thought that, (A), because we are talking about children, there would be much greater sensitivity to this issue as there would be about our treatment and concern for children across the board.

By creating this consciousness of disparity in terms of preparation and capabilities for response with children, in a way, that is a vehicle to alert the entire population and answer some of the questions that have been raised, in general, about our concern for preparedness.

Or I guess in a sentence I can say, if we are very concerned about the welfare of our children in this area, bioprotection, then, surely, if we are going to take steps to advance that kind of capability on behalf of children, the indirect effect as well would be to raise consciousness about the concerns we have for the biothreat, in general.

Mr. PAYNE. Thank you.

Thank you, Madam Chairwoman. Thank you for your indulgence.

Mrs. BROOKS. Thank you. Very, very important question.

I yield 5 minutes to the gentlelady from New York. Thank you for being here.

Ms. CLARKE. Thank you so much, Madam Chairwoman.

I thank our experts this morning, and just wanted to sort of concur with Congressman Pascrell because part of his motivation for his legislation spoke about the petrocorridor and how a bioterrorism attack would impact the immediate population of about 1 million or more residents in New Jersey.

Being his neighbor to the north, coming from New York City, I could see such an event having catastrophic consequences. So I think that this subject matter is something that requires far more attention. I want to thank the leadership here for holding this hearing today.

My first question is to Dr. Kadlec. In 2011, you testified at a joint hearing before the subcommittee on the WMD Prevention and Preparedness Act of 2011 and, at the time, you observed that we had spent about $50 billion on biodefense and that there are legitimate questions as to whether we spent too much in certain areas or overlooked others.

So my question is: Has Federal visibility of biodefense investments improved? If so, how so? If not, how can we get a better idea of where our dollars have been invested and how to prioritize and coordinate future spending?

Dr. KADLEC. Thank you, ma'am, for that question. I think the answer is there has been some improvements and, again, they are kind of buried deep in the bureaucracy.

But one of the issues that occurred, I think, early on in the tenure of the Obama administration was to demand a cross-cutting budget analysis by OMB.

I don't know if that has ever been shared with Congress, but it would certainly be illustrative, maybe, of a better idea of where the money is going and how it is flowing. I think, quite frankly, whether we have spent too much or too little, the question is whether we have spent effectively. That is a big issue, and I will use one example.

One of the great things that Congress did collectively in a bipartisan fashion in 2004 is create the Strategic Reserve Fund, which is also known as BioShield and Project BioShield. With it, it understood very clearly the necessary incentives to have industry basically come to the table and work actively in this space, particularly for countermeasures that don't have commercial—if you will, commercial benefit to their shareholders and to their companies. So that is something that has gone forward.

With the reauthorization of that and with the reauthorization of the Pandemic and All-Hazards Preparedness Act, again, Congress said, "Instead of a 10-year outlay, we will give you a 5-year outlay of approximately $2.6 billion." The challenge is to kind-of get the Government as it stands to appropriate that money and to ask for that money in Presidential budgets and appropriations to—again, to reaffirm the commitment of the Government around it.

So in some ways it is not that we haven't put the money on the table; it is how we put the money on the table and what reassurances we have. That is just one example.

I think there are many other examples where we have been penny-wise and pound-foolish, in hospital preparedness programs where the budget was cut a third this year, or in the metropolitan medical response programs that Representative Payne highlighted.

So I think the thing is that, as the attention to this issue has kind of waned—and Representative Payne talked about the ebbs and flows; it happens in many levels and many different fashions—that is one where we just need to have a consistent level of sustainable funding to ensure that the preparedness that we achieve is something that we can continue and build upon.

Ms. CLARKE. Thank you for your response.

Clearly, the ebb and flow of this does not bode well when you want to remain protected and have a robust infrastructure to deliver.

As I said, I am from New York City and, when you have over 8 million people that have to be attended to in an event, it becomes very challenging if your hospital infrastructure gets overwhelmed and it does not have the capacity. So I can appreciate your response about the funding.

Dr. Inglesby, in your testimony, you note that, over the past 10 years, through significant investment, a cadre of people with expertise and planning for biological terrorism has emerged and a series of major biopreparedness programs have been launched.

In your opinion, are these programs effectively coordinated across various levels of Government and with the private sector?

Dr. INGLESBY. Well, in an enterprise as big as biodefense, I think coordination could always be better and I think communication with industry could always be better. Sometimes I think it is a common refrain to hear from industry that they don't know enough about what the Government wants or in what form it wants it.

So that is a challenge, and it is a challenge for the Federal officials who want to communicate with industry, but also are worried about procurement rules and the way that that operates.

I would say that I am worried about the support of some of the critical programs. You mentioned the budget a moment ago. I think the number $60 billion—in our center, we put out an annual analysis of the biodefense budget. So that number is about in line with what we have calculated that has been spent over time.

But it is a misunderstood number because more than 90 percent of that money is also being spent—it is being spent in the name of biodefense, but it is actually being used for many other purposes, which isn't necessarily a bad thing. It is often a good thing. It's dual-use purposes for research or for preparedness.

But some people will swing around the number like a bludgeon and say, "We've spent $60 billion," but, in reality, what we have spent for biodefense in a dedicated way has been much smaller, much, much smaller.

I am worried that some of the key programs that biodefense planning depends on—the CDC programs, the hospital preparedness programs, the BARDA and BioShield programs—are under a lot of pressure and that, if we continue to erode those problems we will absolutely see a decrease in capability.

So it is important for Congress particularly to know what those key programs are and think a lot about that as they consider their funding choices in the year ahead.

Ms. CLARKE. In both of your responses, I kind of get the feeling that, if you don't use it and maintain it, you lose it, and I think that that is something that we have to be very conscious of as we address these threats that are very present and ever present in our civil society.

I yield back, Madam Chairwoman, and thank you.

Mrs. BROOKS. Thank you.

At this time we will begin the second round of questioning. As I noted in my opening statement, this hearing is part of a series that we plan on taking on of oversight activities on the Federal biosurveillance efforts, particularly BioWatch and NBIC.

Tomorrow, Secretary Johnson comes before the full committee. I am interested in your perspective, specifically on BioWatch, on thoughts with respect to Gen–3, and the NBIC.

Are these initiatives that we are investing significant dollars around the country, are they working, or what changes would you recommend to the new Secretary or to the committee? Dr. Kadlec? I would love to hear from all of you.

Dr. KADLEC. Thank you, Madam Chairwoman.

So subject to the BioWatch program, I have an intimate understanding of the program, having been in the White House at the time of its creation.

I would just point out that the intent of that program was simply to provide public health officials early warning to the risk of a large-scale release of a biological agent. I think that remains as a consistent threat that goes on.

The idea was, though, spiral development of the program as it went on. When the program was first deployed, it was very rudimentary and the idea was that, over time, improvements could be made in an incremental way.

I think there was a decision made—an investment decision made that I think, quite frankly, in retrospect, wasn't probably the wisest one.

We basically took a lot of that investment money and put it against the next generation of BioWatch detectors, and we know the rest of story there at least right now.

So I think, in some ways, BioWatch deserves improvements. BioWatch can be improved by things improving the chronological, if you will, assessment that it can provide when a release occurs. It can also increase the density of collectors.

Certainly there can be improvements subject to the time at which these collectors can be sensed in terms of looking for particles in the atmosphere that could at least trigger a warning or at least an alert to go pull the filters earlier.

So I think there are very substantive things that can be done now. To the idea of an automated system down the road, clearly that is the idealized end-state and clearly that is something that is worthwhile.

But I think sometimes the discussion to date has been a trade-off between environmental detectors and improved clinical diagnosis and the answer is, you can't have either without the other.

So the idea that there is somehow a competing idea out there for clinical diagnostics, point-of-care diagnostics, for example, I think is something that is necessary and invaluable, but you can't eliminate the idea of an environmental detector. I think it is something that we have to continue to work on.

I noticed the idea of anti-ballistic missile defense was one that came in the 1960s and it only occurred decades later in terms of its realization, not because we gave up on it, but we continued to work on it and find the technology to make it work effectively. So, with that, I will just end my comments.

Mrs. BROOKS. Thank you.

Dr. Inglesby.

Dr. INGLESBY. On the two issues, the first on the NBIC program, I think NBIC has had a challenging history. It has had multiple directors over the years and a change in course a number of times.

I would say that I am really pleased with how NBIC has changed over the last year. I think it has garnered a lot more respect in the interagency. I think it has a very strong director.

I know that they have weekly conference calls where all the Federal agencies that are doing biosurveillance get on the phone every week, I think every Friday. I think they have a requirement now that they can convene that group within 60 minutes at the White House's request, and have done so.

I haven't been on the calls; so, I can't speak—you will have to ask the users whether it is valuable to them. But I do think that they have really evolved in a positive direction and are very purposeful and recognize their role as a coordinating entity.

They do a number of other things that are more innovation and local, ground-up surveillance work that I think are pilot projects. But I think their fundamental core is around coordination and I think it is moving in the right direction.

On BioWatch, I do think there is a role for environmental surveillance and I agree with Dr. Kadlec that it should not be zero-sum with clinical diagnostics, which are also vital.

I think the problem with BioWatch in a general sense is that the public health community, which it was built, as Bob says, to inform, in many places don't have a lot of confidence or at least have confidence that they should take action based upon the results. That exists for a number of different reasons, and I am sure the AOA, which I have not seen, probably will go into that.

But I think—if we are going to continue to invest in the BioWatch program or even expand it, I think the public health departments—it is their laboratorians and health officials that are being asked to both do work around it and then trust the results and take action based on it and, if they don't trust it, then they won't act on it and then this will not be a useful investment.

So I think we do have to at a fundamental level build it in concert with that community so that they trust it, understand it and will act on it if there is useful information.

Mrs. BROOKS. Thank you.

Dr. Cole.

Dr. COLE. I would like to comment and add perhaps in the area of BioWatch to the otherwise excellent remarks that we have just heard.

The way I look at it is that the BioWatch ideal is to create a situation that would identify a dangerous biological agent at some location before somebody has symptoms, before anybody actually would be going to a doctor or finding out what would be bothering them or, putting it another way, before the ideal environmental surveillance capability would exist and, in some respects, already does exist, we were all canaries in the coal mine.

The first way you would identify that there had been a biological attack, unless you had advanced warning from the perpetrator, which is unlikely, would be when people start getting sick.

So I very much feel the ideal ought to be respected and that, yes, there have been disappointments in both the speed and the reliability of the detection mechanisms as they have progressed.

But, by all means, I think to forgo continuing efforts to develop research and engineering efforts would be a terrible loss to what I think is an appropriate and attainable end result that we all want, namely, to have effective identification of suspicious organisms when they are actually in the environment and before anybody becomes ill.

Mrs. BROOKS. Thank you so much for that comment.

At this time I would ask unanimous consent to submit to the record the Bio-Response Report Card that we spoke of earlier. Without objection, so ordered.

[The information follows:]

BIO-RESPONSE REPORT CARD

	TREND	SMALL-SCALE NON-CONTAGIOUS	SMALL-SCALE CONTAGIOUS	LARGE-SCALE NON-CONTAGIOUS	LARGE-SCALE CONTAGIOUS	LARGE-SCALE DRUG RESISTANT	GLOBAL CRISIS CONTAGIOUS
DETECTION & DIAGNOSIS	↗	C	C	D	D	F	F
ATTRIBUTION	→	D*	F	F	F	F	F
COMMUNICATION	↗	B	B	C	C	C	C
MEDICAL COUNTERMEASURE AVAILABILITY	↗	B	B	B	D**	F	F
MEDICAL COUNTERMEASURE DEVELOPMENT & APPROVAL PROCESS	→				D		
MEDICAL COUNTERMEASURE DISPENSING	→	B	B	D	D	F	F
MEDICAL MANAGEMENT	→	B	C	D	D	F	F
ENVIRONMENTAL CLEANUP	→	B		F		F	

A	MEETS MOST EXPECTATIONS
B	MEETS MANY EXPECTATIONS
C	MEETS MINIMAL EXPECTATIONS
D	MEETS FEW EXPECTATIONS
F	FAILS TO MEET EXPECTATIONS

ARROWS INDICATE CURRENT TRAJECTORY TOWARD MEETING FUNDAMENTAL EXPECTATIONS (ASSUMES BASELINE FUNDING)

↗ IMPROVING TREND
→ STATUS QUO
↘ DECLINING TREND

* D FOR ANTHRAX, FOR ALL OTHER PATHOGENS AND TOXINS F
** B FOR SMALLPOX

Mrs. BROOKS. At this time, I recognize the gentleman from New Jersey, Mr. Payne, for questions.

Mr. PAYNE. Thank you, Madam Chairwoman.

Just to stay on that topic with the report card, you pointed out the Ds and the Fs. I know, when I brought my report card home and it looked like that, my father would say it is unacceptable. So to that vein, this is absolutely unacceptable, what we see before us.

Mrs. BROOKS. I doubt that ever happened, Mr. Payne.

Mr. PAYNE. The WMD Center Bio-Response Report Card, which we are talking about, released in 2011 gave the Nation a D for its ability to detect and diagnose large-scale attacks, as we have been discussing.

Since 2011, do you think the Nation has made any progress in that category? If so, how, Dr. Kadlec?

Dr. KADLEC. Well, sir, I think the progress is negative at this point. Quite frankly, there are just a lot of—obviously, the economic situation we find ourselves in has put a lot of pressure on a lot of these programs.

I think the attention has moved to other areas, quite frankly, without the kind of oversight from the White House and certainly involvement like your committee's. I think no one is disinterested, but have forgotten about it. We are far away from the events of 2001.

So what I am concerned about is that, as time continues to move forward, many of these fundamental capabilities will ebb away, to use your ebb-and-flow analogy. So I have deep concern about that.

It is very hard to believe that, in today's world, we could be so vulnerable and become more vulnerable than we may be today, but I am very worried about very simple things.

I think Representative Clarke mentioned about the infrastructure—the public health infrastructure. Even though we may have things in the Strategic National Stockpile, we may not be able to get them to the people who need them in time because we don't have the infrastructure and the logistics supply chain in place to do this.

So I am very concerned about this, and I am just so glad that this committee has taken upon itself, along with Representatives King and Pascrell, trying to get the visibility of this issue where it is supposed to be, in the front and center of our National security and homeland security discussions.

Mr. PAYNE. Dr. Inglesby, the Nation received another D for its ability to determine the source of a biological event.

Do you think we have made any progress since 2011 in that respect and, if so, how?

Dr. INGLESBY. I do think that we are continuing to improve, as a whole, microbial science. So we are getting—we do learn more about pathogens and what differentiates them.

I think the problem with biological weapons is that, even if we know exactly what beaker a pathogen is made in, someone could make it in this room and then launch it in India and we wouldn't know that it came from this room.

We may be able to say that it is very much like another bacteria in the same beaker, but you can't attribute a geographic spot to the bacteria itself. So that is always going to be a challenge that lives with us.

It is very different from watching where a missile came from on a map or ballistics from a particular gun. Bacteria can be multiplied. They start in one beaker. They can be put in someone's pocket and moved to another place. I think that is going to be a fundamental challenge for us and we are going to have to rely on different kinds of things to figure out the source.

Mr. PAYNE. Dr. Cole, how do you think we can improve around these issues our capabilities?

Dr. COLE. Well, the bottom line obviously is continuing research and development. I would add this, though, to the general conversation.

Before 9/11 in 2001, there was very, very little thought about a multiple number of airplanes being hijacked and crashed into buildings virtually at the same time, simultaneously.

Before the anthrax letters were sent, there were very, very few people and none in the United States Government that I am aware of who had actually projected among the many possible means of delivery of a biological agent as a weapon sending spores through the mail.

By coincidence, about 8 or 10 months before the actual anthrax letters were sent there was an experiment up in Canada and it did indicate that these spores could spread and leak from envelopes, but nothing on a large-scale measure as what we faced, which I guess answers—is a very unfortunate answer, but an accurate one.

We don't know altogether how and in what manner the next attack on us—whether biological or otherwise—could be. It could well be in a manner that none of us have imagined or been creative about. So we do need generic bases for concern.

So on that basis, I would—in picking up with what Dr. Inglesby just said, I wouldn't worry as much about the source. Yes, it is not nice to get a D or certainly an F in any course you take.

I would be much more interested in what we can do about intercepting once the source or once the distribution or the release of biological agents have taken place.

So I am very much concerned about response—preparedness for response as well as identification early on where the material came from.

Mr. PAYNE. Thank you, sir.

Mrs. BROOKS. Thank you.

The Chairwoman now recognizes the gentlelady from New York for questions.

Ms. CLARKE. Thank you very much, Madam Chairwoman.

Picking up on Dr. Cole's last comment, I would like to ask Dr. Kadlec—there are numerous and unique challenges related to detecting and responding to a WMD attack, especially bioterror attacks.

What do you think that Congress can do to ensure that first responders, emergency services personnel are effectively prepared to respond during a biological attack? How can these people be best utilized during a response?

Dr. KADLEC. Thank you for that question.

I would just simply say we need to protect our first responders and their families. Simple as that. We have the means to do so today in many respects in terms of vaccines that we have in our stockpile as well as the ability to basically develop antibiotic kits that can be kept at home safely and securely to ensure that, should there be an emergency requiring our first responders and every first responder to respond—because, as we heard from Representative Pascrell, these are not going to be small events, potentially.

These are going to be very large events affecting several hundred thousand—millions of people, in New York, 8 million. So you would like to believe that every fireman, every policemen, every public health worker, every sanitation worker who is going to be needed to man pods, maybe every postal worker who in some jurisdictions are going to deliver antibiotics to the general public, have the means to protect themselves and their family and the confidence they can go out into that environment and do their duty without concern for themselves or their family members.

Ms. CLARKE. So old habits die hard. One of the challenges around the 9/11 event is that the instinct of the responder is to go and respond irregardless of what the dangers may be to that individual.

What type of measures need to be put in place to really do the type of behavior modification that enables our responders to do their work effectively and not have the ripple effects that we have seen as a result of just their instincts?

Dr. KADLEC. Thank you, ma'am.

I would just recall Dr. Cole's comments early on in his statement about the vital importance of education and training. That is transformational in the sense of how we would raise awareness and, if you will, give our first responders and the public, in general, information they could use in those kind of circumstances.

I think one of the great issues—and it was talked about earlier—are the psychological effects of biological warfare insofar as, in some ways, they prey on the worst ruminations of people's minds.

In some ways, you can dispel a lot of those concerns and at least inform people in a way that they do have control of their environment and there are things substantively they can do to protect themselves and their families.

Ms. CLARKE. My question to you would be—and to the entire panel is: Is there evidence in the training academies across this Nation from the municipal on up that this type of adjustment is being made?

You know, as we sit here, graduating classes, the training that is taking place, you know, are they playing from the old playbook or have you seen an integration of practices that would protect them?

Dr. KADLEC. Well, ma'am, I can't comment broadly, other than to say that I believe—in the professional education and training areas, particularly within the medical public health areas, I don't believe that they are institutionalized in a way that bring the best practices to care for people in a WMD environment.

I think there were some earnest efforts after 9/11. Those efforts haven't been sustained. They have become somewhat fragmented. They are not part of the course load of any given curricula, I believe, in any profession, whether it be physicians, nurses.

I would just say that EMS is probably the best position to date. They have generally instituted many of these ideas and curricula changes.

But I believe that we are far from where we need to be in basically having everyone have a basis of understanding of what to do in a disaster, whether it be a WMD event or even a natural event, for that matter.

Ms. CLARKE. Dr. Cole.

Dr. COLE. If I could add something, it is sort of an advertisement plug, I guess.

At the school at which I am an adjunct professor of emergency medicine, there is a course being taught for the first time, to my knowledge, in any American medical school on terror medicine, which deals with the unique aspects and distinctive aspects that apply to responding to a terror event.

Now, there is a lot of overlap with disaster medicine and emergency medicine. But when one looks carefully, there are a whole series of issues, including how one has to deal with a biological agent used for hostile purposes, that would not apply otherwise.

So, yes, there are spots. But to your question, which is very important—why and how widespread is training appropriate?—I don't think we know. I don't think there has been an adequate recent survey on what is being taught, if anything, about these areas.

But I did refer in my oral statement and written remarks to the fact that a recent poll of hundreds of pediatricians in the State of Michigan—after the surveyors looked at this, they concluded that 85 percent of them had not had any serious training and that, in general, these people were totally unprepared for a biological event.

Ms. CLARKE. Thank you very much, Madam Chairwoman.

Mrs. BROOKS. Thank you, as always, for your concern for our first responders. I very much appreciate that.

I have one last question that I would ask each of you to help us, which I think would also help Congressman Pascrell and Congressman King.

As we try to elevate the importance of this continued discussion and focus on bioterrorism, how can we do a better job in describing what the impact is?

So when you are educating people, whether it is in classrooms or whether it's at a dinner party, about bioterrorism, do you have a way to help us describe what a horrific significant impact a bioterrorism attack would have on our country and our citizens?

Anyone want to jump in to give us the elevator speech, so to speak, to help us explain the importance of this topic as to what the impact might be? Dr. Kadlec.

Dr. KADLEC. Well, I would just simply say the elevator speech I would use is basically the United States demonstrated in the 1950s and 1960s the plausibility of this form of warfare.

It became so significant in our concerns that we tried to eliminate it as an acceptable form of warfare by basically engaging in a treaty with a number of nation-states, the Biologic Weapons Convention, and certainly our worst fears were realized when we recognized that other nations could assume this capability and certainly terrorists.

So we have empowered now individuals, groups of individuals, with the ability to kill as many people as a nuclear weapon and they can do so at a fraction of the cost without the technical burdens or liabilities associated with nuclear weapons.

I think that should be a chilling—chilling story for any person who lives in a major metropolitan area, like Representative Clarke, or in the corridor, as Representative Payne, or Madam Chairwoman, even in Indianapolis.

I believe that no part of the country could be spared from this, and I think that is the issue that has to be conveyed, is that we are all vulnerable.

The fact of the matter is that there are substantive things that we can do to reduce our vulnerability. We can't eliminate it. We can reduce our vulnerability in a way that would basically at least make this a manageable risk, not an unmanageable risk, as it is today.

Mrs. BROOKS. Thank you.

Dr. Inglesby.

Dr. INGLESBY. I guess in my elevator speech I would say it is important for those who don't remember it to recall that a series of letters containing anthrax which led to less than 10 deaths nearly paralyzed our Federal Government and put the Nation on edge for months and that those bioattacks were delivered in the crudest imaginable form and that technology now exists to create and to disseminate biological weapons on a scale that is far, far greater than what we experienced in 2001.

Our strongest defense is to become resilient and prepared for those kinds of attacks. It is in our capability to do that, but we have to actually plan for it and do it.

Mrs. BROOKS. Thank you very much, Dr. Cole.

Dr. COLE. If this were a very long elevator ride——

Mrs. BROOKS. I understand you have a train to catch; so, it may have to be a short elevator ride.

Dr. COLE. Not only would I incorporate—or try to synopsize what we just heard from Dr. Kadlec and Dr. Inglesby, I would make two additional points.

One is that, unlike any other weapon, we are all familiar at some level with the effects of infectious disease. All of us have had colds. Many have had flu and others.

One can remember—certainly in my own family, in my own mind, I can remember some very serious consequences, maybe not critical, but enough to know that this is not a pleasant thing.

Can one then imagine becoming infected by something that was intended to cause you not only to become ill, but possibly to die? There is a culture kind of connection to this, to biologicals, that we don't have in another areas of hostility and weaponry.

Second, I would speak to the moral question, the moral issue. The Biological Weapons Convention treaty that prohibits the use or even the development or stockpiling of biological weapons was first put on the table in 1972, and it contains a unique phrase that I think all of us ought to treasure as to its wording: "The use of these kinds of weapons"—and I am quoting from this convention— "is repugnant to the conscience of mankind."

That was the first treaty that ever used that kind of language, that really elevated the moral and ethical issue to the point where it has, I think, a personal and a psychological effect, because it was the forerunner of then continuing usage of ethics and morality in other treaties as well.

So I would emphasize those points, particularly the familiarity we all have with moderately effective biological agents, and then how important it is for us as a society to be aware of how awful this kind of thing is, which, in effect, indirectly can minimize the likelihood of its use.

Even those societies, civilizations, countries that have no moral compunctions about using biological weapons would then understand that, for many in the world, whatever the purpose of their aggressiveness or bad behavior would be, it would be so repulsive that it could act as an additional deterrent to them wanting to use it in the first place.

Thank you.

Mrs. BROOKS. Thank you very much. I think that is an appropriate way to conclude today's hearing.

I want to thank each you for dedicating your careers to this incredibly important topic to our country and to mankind, as you so eloquently stated, Dr. Cole. I want to thank the staff for getting such incredible witnesses before the subcommittee.

We will do our best to continue to move this discussion forward. The Members of the subcommittee may have additional questions for you and will ask you to respond to these questions in writing.

Pursuant to Committee Rule 7(e), the hearing record would be open for 10 days.

Without objection, the subcommittee stands adjourned.

[Whereupon, at 11:40 a.m., the subcommittee was adjourned.]

APPENDIX

Question 1. Our country has been subjected to numerous, potentially catastrophic biohazard exposures in recent years in our agricultural industry; the outbreak of the H1N1 (Swine Flu) and the H5N1 (Bird Flu) viruses come to mind. Fortunately, none of these exposures have resulted in any large-scale damage.

However, agro-terrorism, which is the malicious use of plant or animal pathogens to cause devastating disease in the agricultural sector, is a concern. But it doesn't stop there. Natural or accidental biological events can have the same devastating impacts as those which are intentionally caused.

To give you a scenario, in 2001, Foot & Mouth Disease affected 9,000 farms in the United Kingdom and required the destruction of more than 4 million cows. USDA researchers believe that a similar outbreak in the United States would cost taxpayers up to $60 billion. Given the relative size of the United States to the United Kingdom, this could result in the need to destroy 20 million head of cattle in a short period of time with little advance notice.

Does the Federal Government have a plan in place and the attendant resources to handle a disaster of this magnitude? Please identify with specificity this plan and those dedicated resources of people and equipment. Specifically, how would the decomposing and potentially infectious carcasses be disposed of? How quickly would this response occur, and what would its effectiveness be?

Answer. Response was not received at the time of publication.

Question 2. What is the Federal Government's response plan for a large-scale avian influenza outbreak in the poultry industry? Specifically, how would the diseased and infectious birds be disposed of? How quickly would this response occur, and what would its effectiveness be?

Answer. Response was not received at the time of publication.

Question 3. When a natural or man-caused biological event occurs in the homeland and that affects our livestock or other agricultural interest, we need to ensure we have a comprehensive, pre-planned, pre-resourced, and pre-positioned response plan in place.

What recommendations would you make to FEMA to ensure our agricultural interests are protected and that we are prepared to respond in the event of a agro-terrorist attack or an epidemic?

Answer. Response was not received at the time of publication.

Question 1. Our country has been subjected to numerous, potentially catastrophic biohazard exposures in recent years in our agricultural industry; the outbreak of the H1N1 (Swine Flu) and the H5N1 (Bird Flu) viruses come to mind. Fortunately, none of these exposures have resulted in any large scale damage.

However, agro-terrorism, which is the malicious use of plant or animal pathogens to cause devastating disease in the agricultural sector, is a concern. But it doesn't stop there. Natural or accidental biological events can have the same devastating impacts as those which are intentionally caused.

To give you a scenario, in 2001, Foot & Mouth Disease affected 9,000 farms in the United Kingdom and required the destruction of more than 4 million cows. USDA researchers believe that a similar outbreak in the United States would cost taxpayers up to $60 billion. Given the relative size of the United States to the United Kingdom, this could result in the need to destroy 20 million head of cattle in a short period of time with little advance notice.

Does the Federal Government have a plan in place and the attendant resources to handle a disaster of this magnitude? Please identify with specificity this plan and those dedicated resources of people and equipment. Specifically, how would the decomposing and potentially infectious carcasses be disposed of? How quickly would this response occur, and what would its effectiveness be?

Question 2. What is the Federal Government's response plan for a large-scale avian influenza outbreak in the poultry industry? Specifically, how would the diseased and infectious birds be disposed of? How quickly would this response occur, and what would its effectiveness be?

Question 3. When a natural or man-caused biological event occurs in the homeland and that affects our livestock or other agricultural interest, we need to ensure we have a comprehensive, pre-planned, pre-resourced, and pre-positioned response plan in place.

What recommendations would you make to FEMA to ensure our agricultural interests are protected and that we are prepared to respond in the event of a agro-terrorist attack or an epidemic?

Answer. Belated thank you for the follow-up email and the questions from Congressman Palazzo. Those are all very important questions, and I would have liked to have been able to address them.

But unfortunately neither I nor my colleagues at the UPMC Center for Health Security have the expertise or backgrounds to be able to answer those questions competently. Our Center has a focus preventing and responding to threats to human health, and we don't have animal health experts on staff. I am sorry that I am not of any assistance in responding to them.

QUESTIONS FROM HONORABLE STEVEN M. PALAZZO FOR LEONARD A. COLE

Question 1. Our country has been subjected to numerous, potentially catastrophic biohazard exposures in recent years in our agricultural industry; the outbreak of the H1N1 (Swine Flu) and the H5N1 (Bird Flu) viruses come to mind. Fortunately, none of these exposures have resulted in any large scale damage.

However, agro-terrorism, which is the malicious use of plant or animal pathogens to cause devastating disease in the agricultural sector, is a concern. But it doesn't stop there. Natural or accidental biological events can have the same devastating impacts as those which are intentionally caused.

To give you a scenario, in 2001, Foot & Mouth Disease affected 9,000 farms in the United Kingdom and required the destruction of more than 4 million cows. USDA researchers believe that a similar outbreak in the United States would cost taxpayers up to $60 billion. Given the relative size of the United States to the United Kingdom, this could result in the need to destroy 20 million head of cattle in a short period of time with little advance notice.

Does the Federal Government have a plan in place and the attendant resources to handle a disaster of [great] magnitude? Specifically, how would the decomposing and potentially infectious carcasses be disposed of? How quickly would this response occur, and what would its effectiveness be?

Answer.* Since the United States has not experienced a catastrophic outbreak of Foot and Mouth Disease or other livestock disease in recent memory, response plans are based largely on extrapolations from routine disposal methods and lessons from major outbreaks elsewhere, specifically in Europe and Taiwan. A review by the U.S. Department of Agriculture (USDA) indicates four principal methods of disposal of infectious carcasses: Burial (on-site), incineration, rendering (conversion to other products), and composting (breakdown into fertilizer).

---

*[Note.—My bioterrorism expertise is largely focused on the direct effects on people, not plants or animals. In providing answers to the questions I have searched Government websites and other literature. I also benefited from conversation with veterinary expert Dr. Sandra San Miguel, Associate Dean of Engagement at Purdue University. Before addressing the posed questions, I note that protection regarding any outbreak of animal disease involves layers of interested parties. Federal law requires that serious animal diseases, such as Foot and Mouth Disease, be reported immediately. Federal oversight is largely under the purview of the U.S. Department of Agriculture (USDA) and its Animal and Plant Health Inspection Service (APHIS). States also maintain agencies responsible for oversight and control of animal disease outbreaks.

For livestock events involving reportable diseases the emergency response is Federal first (led by APHIS), and then local assistance is used. For responses involving natural emergencies (flood, tornado, etc.) the response usually goes local first. If local resources become exhausted Federal aid is sought.

Personal and economic interests buttress the likelihood of early reporting. The following parties are positioned and obliged to report disease as soon as recognized: Veterinarians, farmers, slaughter facilities, truckers and other transporters, Federal and State plant inspectors, even 4-H youngsters—in short, everyone in the livestock industry. Given this array, Dr. San Miguel believes that any clinical signs of disease would be recognized quickly. However, before such signs are visible, an infected animal may already have been exposed to other animals.]

Strengths and limitations are associated with each method. Burial of numerous carcasses in large pits can be relatively quick, though inadequate protective treatment and insulation (with chemicals and barriers) around the pit risks soil and groundwater pollution.

Contained incineration can be effective but the number and availability of enclosed incinerators is limited. Open-air burning, while quick, contaminates surrounding air. Rendering and composting requires transporting numerous carcasses perhaps to distant facilities, which also are limited in numbers. Carcass disposal options are more fully reviewed in a 2004 report by the National Agricultural Biosecurity Center at Kansas State University. (*https://krex.k-state.edu/dspace/handle/2097/662*)

I am unaware of a Federal plan to dispose of carcasses explicitly resulting from a catastrophic disease outbreak. Oversight responsibility for this would fall to the USDA's Animal and Plant Health Inspection Service. The response presumably would be a ramping up of existing methods as suggested by an observation in a USDA publication: "Past experiences of epidemic disease outbreaks in Taiwan and Europe indicate that use of several disposal methods in combination may be required to deal with catastrophic mortality disposal." ("Swine Carcass Disposal Options for Routine and Catastrophic Mortality," Council for Agricultural Science and Technology (CAST), Issue Paper No. 39, U.S. Department of Agriculture, July 2008.)

Question 2. What is the Federal Government's response plan for a large-scale avian influenza outbreak in the poultry industry? Specifically, how would the diseased and infectious birds be disposed of? How quickly would this response occur, and what would its effectiveness be?

Answer. Unlike for livestock, and particularly large animals, disposal of birds infected with avian influenza should not include burial. The virus is highly contagious and burial and land containment cannot be sufficiently controlled to preclude its spread to other birds or mammals. Thus, incineration is the method of choice. But because of the virus's high infectivity potential, transporting birds to standard apparatus such as solid municipal waste incinerators or autoclaves is not advised. Rather, portable (truck driven) "refractory walled" fire boxes are deemed the most suitable to dispose of suspect bird carcasses. (Avian Influenza Bird Carcass Disposal, Disposal of Culled Birds and Dead Wild Birds at Remote Locations, USDA Animal Welfare Information Center, *http://www.airburners.com/DATA-FILES__Print/AB-Bird__Flu__%20Carcass__Disposal-v0306d.pdf*)

The speed and effectiveness of disposal, like response capabilities in other areas of disaster management, doubtless vary from one location to another. Some areas will have quicker access to the required equipment, more appropriate personnel, and perhaps have undertaken more frequent and realistic preparedness exercises.

Question 3. When a natural or man-caused biological event occurs in the homeland and that affects our livestock or other agricultural interest, we need to ensure we have a comprehensive, pre-planned, pre-resourced, and pre-positioned response plan in place.

What recommendations would you make to FEMA to ensure our agricultural interests are protected and that we are prepared to respond in the event of a agroterrorist attack or an epidemic?

Answer. For every disease of concern, the USDA's Animal and Plant Health Inspection Service (APHIS) has plans in place including provision of medications, euthanasia, and personnel protection. The Federal Emergency Management Agency (FEMA) should be working with APHIS in furtherance of these and other response methods. According to Dr. San Miguel, this cooperation exists at the State level in Indiana and elsewhere.

For example, the lead oversight agency in Iowa is the State's Department of Agriculture and Land Stewardship (IDALS), which includes a network of 330 veterinary and animal health professionals trained to respond to disease emergencies in the State. The IDALS response plans explicitly include working with the Federal DOA–APHIS. (*http://www.cfsph.iastate.edu/Animal__Response/English/pdf/A4__SPN-__BusinessOverview.pdf*)

Gauging cooperation at the Federal level between DOA–APHIS and FEMA would require further inquiries into activities of the two agencies and of other relevant bodies.

○

www.ingramcontent.com/pod-product-compliance
Lightning Source LLC
Chambersburg PA
CBHW081757280526
45789CB00008B/2887

Testimony

Before the Subcommittee on Oversight and Investigations, Committee on Energy and Commerce, House of Representatives

For Release on Delivery
Expected at 10:00 a.m. ET
Wednesday, June 25, 2014

MEDICARE FRAUD

Further Actions Needed to Address Fraud, Waste, and Abuse

Statement of Kathleen M. King
Director, Health Care

GAO Highlights

Highlights of GAO-14-712T, a testimony before the Subcommittee on Oversight and Investigations, Committee on Energy and Commerce, House of Representatives

June 25, 2014

MEDICARE FRAUD

Further Actions Needed to Address Fraud, Waste, and Abuse

Why GAO Did This Study

GAO has designated Medicare as a high-risk program, in part because the program's size and complexity make it vulnerable to fraud, waste, and abuse. In 2013, Medicare financed health care services for approximately 51 million individuals at a cost of about $604 billion. The deceptive nature of fraud makes its extent in the Medicare program difficult to measure in a reliable way, but it is clear that fraud contributes to Medicare's fiscal problems. More broadly, in fiscal year 2013, CMS estimated that improper payments—some of which may be fraudulent—were almost $50 billion.

This statement focuses on the progress made and important steps to be taken by CMS and its program integrity contractors to reduce fraud in Medicare. This statement is based on relevant GAO products and recommendations issued from 2004 through 2014 using a variety of methodologies. Additionally, in June 2014, GAO updated information based on new regulations regarding enrollment of certain providers in Medicare by examining public documents.

View GAO-14-712T. For more information, contact Kathleen M. King at (202) 512-7114 or kingk@gao.gov.

What GAO Found

The Centers for Medicare & Medicaid Services (CMS)—the agency within the Department of Health and Human Services (HHS) that oversees Medicare—has made progress in implementing several key strategies GAO identified or recommended in prior work as helpful in protecting Medicare from fraud; however, implementing other important actions that GAO recommended could help CMS and its program integrity contractors combat fraud. These strategies are:

Provider and Supplier Enrollment: The Patient Protection and Affordable Care Act (PPACA) authorized, and CMS has implemented, actions to strengthen provider and supplier enrollment that address past weaknesses identified by GAO and HHS's Office of Inspector General. For example, CMS has hired contractors to determine whether providers and suppliers have valid licenses and are at legitimate locations. CMS could further strengthen enrollment screening by issuing a rule to require additional provider and supplier disclosures of information, such as any suspension of payments from a federal health care program, and establishing core elements for provider and supplier compliance programs, as authorized by PPACA.

Prepayment and Postpayment Claims Review: Medicare uses prepayment review to deny claims that should not be paid and postpayment review to recover improperly paid claims. GAO has found that increased use of prepayment edits could help prevent improper Medicare payments. For example, prior GAO work identified millions of dollars of payments that appeared to be inconsistent with selected coverage and payment policies and therefore improper. Postpayment reviews are also critical to identifying and recouping overpayments. GAO recommended better oversight of both (1) the information systems analysts use to identify claims for postpayment review, in a 2011 report, and (2) the contractors responsible for these reviews, in a 2013 report. CMS has taken action or has actions under way to address these recommendations.

Addressing Identified Vulnerabilities: Having mechanisms in place to resolve vulnerabilities that could lead to improper payments is critical to effective program management and could help address fraud. However, prior GAO work has shown weaknesses in CMS's processes to address such vulnerabilities. For example, GAO has made multiple recommendations to CMS to remove Social Security numbers from beneficiaries' Medicare cards to help prevent identity theft. HHS agreed with these recommendations, but reported that CMS could not proceed with the changes for a variety of reasons, including funding limitations, and therefore has not taken action.

GAO work under way addressing these key strategies includes examining: (1) how well CMS's information system can prevent and detect the continued enrollment of ineligible or potentially fraudulent providers and suppliers in Medicare, (2) the potential use of electronic-card technologies to help reduce Medicare fraud, (3) CMS's oversight of program integrity efforts for prescription drugs, and (4) CMS's oversight of some of the contractors that conduct reviews of claims after payment. These studies could help CMS more systematically reduce potential fraud in the Medicare program.

_____ United States Government Accountability Office